BY THE EDITORS OF CONSUMER GUIDE®

Car Spotter's Encyclopedia 1940~1980

BEEKMAN HOUSE
New York

Car Spotter's Encyclopedia 1940~1980

Copyright© 1982 by Publications International, Ltd.
All rights reserved.
This book may not be reproduced or quoted in whole or in part by mimeograph or any other printed means or for presentation on radio or television without written permission from:

Louis Weber, President
Publications International, Ltd.
3841 West Oakton Street
Skokie, Illinois 60076

Permission is never granted for commercial purposes.

Library of Congress Catalog Card Number: 81-82597
ISBN: 0-517-352044

This edition published by:
Beekman House
Distributed by Crown Publishers, Inc.
One Park Avenue
New York, New York 10016

Manufactured in the United States of America
10 9 8 7 6 5 4 3 2 1

CONTENTS

CONTENTS

Acknowledgements

The generosity and hard work of many individuals and organizations made it possible to include more than 3000 photographs and illustrations in *Car Spotter's Encyclopedia 1940-1980.* Contributing artists were Theodore Alexander, Darlene Bock, Tim Burkhardt, Tim Clemens, Richard Flory, Thom Joris, James Kust, and Herb Slobin. Photographs were obtained from George Domer, Jeffrey I. Godshall, Asa Hall, Phil Hall, Richard M. Langworth, Richard Quinn, American Motors Corp., Avanti Motor Corp., Checker Motors Corp., Chrysler Corp., Excalibur Automobile Corp., Ford Motor Co., General Motors Corp., and the Motor Vehicle Manufacturers Association.

Back in the '20s, the easiest way to tell one make of car from another was by the shape of its radiator. Today, there are those who say they can't tell a Chevrolet from a Ford unless they're close enough to read the nameplates. Whether today's cars are truly less distinctive than their predecessors is a debatable point. But one thing's for sure: In the more than 75 years since Henry Ford started selling his Model T "in any color you want as long as it's black," American automobiles have undergone tremendous change. *Car Spotter's Encyclopedia 1940-1980* is a graphic, chronological record of that change. But it's more than just a record. The thousands of detailed line drawings and photographs presented here tell the story of why some automakers succeeded and why others didn't.

If you had to credit one individual with making appearance a significant factor in the automobile business, it would have to be Alfred P. Sloan of General Motors. Sloan was an astute observer of human nature with a natural gift for merchandising. He saw early on that the more affordable, the more universal cars became, the more people would be attracted to cars that looked new and distinctive. After all, this was the country where making a good impression and keeping up with the Joneses were national passions.

Sloan made appearance an important tool for boosting car sales in the mid-'20s. By 1927, his more modern, more colorful Chevrolet was outselling the Model T Ford, which Henry had stubbornly refused to change substantially in nearly 19 years. That, plus Dearborn's lengthy changeover to the Model A, enabled Chevy to pass Ford in total production for the first time that year. And in the next 45 years, Chevy would relinquish the number-one spot only three times.

The Model T, of course, put the nation on wheels. As the first car built on a mass-production assembly line, it could be made in such huge numbers that it could be sold at unheard-of prices—as little as $260 by 1925. Ford had transformed the automobile from a plaything for the rich to an affordable means of transportation for the common man. Yet there were still many cars—particularly luxury makes like Packard, Lincoln, Pierce, Auburn, Stutz, and Cadillac—that continued to be made the old-fashioned way. They were painstakingly assembled, with bodywork constructed separately by coachbuilders using time-honored techniques left over

from the days of the carriage makers. Naturally, such cars were expensive, but these great "Classics" of the '20s and '30s embodied what some critics still consider the peak of automotive design. Ironically, it was during this era that carefully considered design began to be applied to less exclusive, mass-production cars.

The first automotive stylist was probably a young artist named Harley Earl. The son of a carriage maker, Earl had made a name for himself on the West Coast as chief designer for the Don Lee studio, then one of the prominent custom-body purveyors to the elite. Cadillac General Manager Lawrence P. Fisher was so impressed with Earl's total approach to car design that he signed him on in early 1926 to work as a consultant in Detroit. Earl's first project: the 1927 LaSalle, which would be the first volume car to be deliberately styled in the modern sense. Soon after that, Earl was invited by Alfred Sloan to work for GM full-time and was given the specific task of setting up an in-house design department. This was duly organized as the "Art and Colour Section" (the English spelling for color was used for a touch of snob appeal). It was an industry first that would soon be copied by other auto companies. After the 1927 LaSalle, the professional hand of the stylist became increasingly evident in the shape of American cars.

Earl was a pioneer in his profession. For example, he began the use of modeling clay to evolve the form of various body components—and in the late '20s, clay was considered a highly unusual material for this purpose. Also, he created *complete* designs. The main body, hood, fenders, lights, and other parts were always developed in relation to each other so as to blend into a unified whole. This was in contrast to most custom-body makers, who usually worked from the cowl back while leaving a car's "stock" hood, radiator, and headlamps pretty much as they came from the factory.

While coachbuilders like LeBaron, Dietrich, Darrin, Brunn, Willoughby, Rollson, and others were creating the Classics, others were moving away from the traditional, square-rigged lines descended from the first horseless carriages. They began to experiment with streamlining, a design ideal inspired by the Art Deco school and aircraft construction principles, both of which were having a great impact on industrial design. It took a while for the public to get used to streamlined cars, as Chrysler discovered to its financial peril with the Airflow. Yet sleek streamlined designs like Tom Tjaarda's 1933 Lincoln-Zephyr or Gordon Buehrig's now-revered Cord 810 had widespread influence.

By 1940, the basic design principles to be followed in the postwar period were firmly established and accepted. Running boards were disappearing as bodies were made wider. Headlamps began to merge into the front fenders, which in turn were being blended together with the hood. The separate, detachable trunk was absorbed into the body as a structural component. Fabric roof inserts were abandoned in favor of all-steel "turret" tops. "Pontoon" fenders that fully surrounded the

1927 LaSalle Series 303 roadster

wheels appeared, shaped to enhance the impression of length and power. Grilles became less vertical to increase the illusion of width. Yet despite such changes, some of the finest expressions of "classic" design appeared in 1940-42: the senior Packards and Series 75 Cadillacs, both with majestic proportions, as well as Edsel Ford's beautifully conceived Lincoln Continental and the last production LaSalle.

It's interesting to speculate how American styling might have progressed had car production not been interrupted by World War II. When they could spare time from defense work, designers at Chrysler, Ford, and General Motors all toyed with sketches and clay models for postwar cars. Many of these were photographed. Those pictures that survive today show that these proposals were mostly extensions of earlier ideas, not that radically different. Ultimately, they were discarded. The automakers realized that once war ended there would be a car-starved public eager to buy almost anything, even cars that were little more than warmed-over prewar models. Thus, it's not surprising that the first postwar cars were precisely that. Besides, the quickest and cheapest way for Detroit to convert from war work to civilian production—and to capitalize on the great pent-up buyer demand—was to use prewar tooling. This proved beneficial for the designers. For some three years, between the end of 1945 and the end of 1948, they were able to devote all their time to newer and more advanced concepts than the ones they'd come up with in the war years, when they could work on such things only occasionally. So in a sense, World War II advanced automotive styling, perhaps by a good five years.

The interesting exception to this was Studebaker. That company relied primarily on a consultant group headed by Raymond Loewy. With little wartime work to worry about, the Loewy team was free to work on new postwar Studebaker proposals. Predictably, South Bend got the jump on everyone else by a good two years with its brand-new 1947 models, the first truly new postwar design and the one that made some people wonder, "Which way is it going?" It was not the last time Studebaker would be an industry style leader, but it was perhaps the last opportunity the company had to capitalize fully on its lead. Sadly, it didn't.

From the design standpoint, the 1949 model year is historic, perhaps the most significant single model year ever. There are two reasons for this. First, all-new postwar models appeared under virtually every major nameplate (save Studebaker and Kaiser-Frazer), one of the few times that's happened in Detroit history. Second, these cars ushered in design trends that would be followed in the '50s and would evolve into the cars of the '60s and '70s. The use of styling as the key ingredient in the annual model change (later derisively termed "planned obsolescence") also dates from this benchmark year. From then on, car styling would be altered frequently, sometimes radically. Most often this was change purely for the sake of change, but there was also change prompted by shifts in buyer tastes and

needs. And some styling features, like the wraparound windshield, the lower hood, and the pillarless "hardtop-convertible," were made possible only by the advent of new engineering and materials technology.

As an example of the dynamic metamorphosis in American postwar car design, let's briefly review the design history of a single make, the standard Ford, from 1949 to 1980. The 1949 Ford was the most dramatically different car from Dearborn in a generation. It was more compact outside than the prewar-based 1946-48 design, yet roomier inside and totally modern in appearance by the standards of the day. Its basic shape was the work of Richard Caleal, working under the aegis of design consultant George Walker, and was somewhat influenced by Caleal's earlier work at Studebaker. The fenders on the '49 were completely integral with the body, the slab-sided look popular at the time. It was lower than earlier Fords, too. Its full-width grille was set off by a distinctive bullet suggestive of an airplane propeller. Hood and front fenders were still recognizably separate elements, but were more unified than on any previous Ford.

The '49 design proved very successful and gave Ford its first truly profitable sales year since the late '30s. Ford was a year behind rival Chevrolet with a true hardtop, but joined the fray with the Victoria, styled by Gordon Buehrig, for the 1951 model year, the last season for the original '49 design.

A complete body change was decreed for 1952. This brought a longer wheelbase, reduced overall height, and greater width—the longer-lower-wider syndrome that would afflict Detroit for the next 15 years. The '52 hood was flatter and less distinct from the front fenders than on the 1949-51 Ford. Overall contours were somewhat boxy but clean, and the slab sides were relieved at the rear by modest sheetmetal ridges that jutted forward to suggest motion. This design generation stayed mostly the same through 1954. Grilles again featured a central bullet theme.

Another major style change appeared for 1955, and produced the flashiest Fords yet. The grille was lower and concave, with prominent parking lamps either side and a deep bumper below. Ford adopted the wrap-around windshield for the first time, an idea begun with several GM show cars in 1953. For the new top-line Fairlane series, Ford applied a distinctive chrome sweep-spear that began at the top of the peaked headlight brows and then curved down to run along the bodysides to the rear. It served as a convenient division for the optional two-tone paint schemes that were already very popular with buyers. The most striking of the '55s was doubtless the new Crown Victoria, a two-door sedan decorated with a wide chrome band that wrapped over the roof from one B-post to the other. A green-tinted Plexiglas transparent panel forward of the band could be ordered, an idea introduced a year earlier on the Skyliner hardtop.

After a mild facelift for '56, Ford again restyled, fielding four separate series on two wheelbases. Hood and front fenders were now completely integrated, and prominently hooded headlamps were thrust out over a simple grid grille. Windshields got a more severe dogleg angle at the A-pillar. The same basic design returned for '58 with more glitter and flash. The grille was styled to blend in with the front bumper, and four smaller headlamps appeared where two had been before, following the industry's switch to quads started the year before. A substantial restyle for '59 brought flatter front fenders and an even lower and wider grille with an insert composed of tiny starlike elements.

Ford's next new bodyshell arrived for 1960. It would have a fairly long life, lasting through 1964. The 1960 front end was marked by a broad hoodline sloped down slightly to the grille, which now contained the headlamps. Front fenders had prominent ridges or peaks that continued along the bodysides to terminate in horizontal tailfins. Ford didn't sprout vertical wings in the '50s and early '60s like Chrysler Corporation products did, a reflection perhaps of division general manager Robert S. MacNamara's sober, conservative tastes. Ford grilles in these years alternated between simple concave affairs on the '61 and '63 and the more complicated grid of the '62 and the wavy bar treatment on the '64.

Meanwhile, Ford was introducing companion lines to satisfy specific groups of buyers, a proliferation of model sizes and types that would sweep the industry in the '60s. The four-seat Thunderbird had appeared for 1958, replacing the original 1955-57 two-seater. One of its distinctive styling features, a flat roof with wide rear quarter pillars, was applied to the full-size Ford beginning with the 1959 Galaxie series to give the big cars a visual link with the personal-luxury T-Bird. The cleanly styled Falcon arrived for 1960 as one of the Big Three compacts designed to battle the increasingly popular small foreign models like the Volkswagen Beetle. The Falcon's bodyside sculpturing was quite similar to that of the big '60 Ford. Then came the Fairlane for 1962, the first of what would be called intermediate-size cars. Its grille was obviously related to that year's big Ford.

1948 Super DeLuxe convertible

1955 Fairlane Crown Victoria hardtop coupe

1950 Custom V8 convertible

1956 Fairlane Sunliner convertible

1952 Crestline Sunliner convertible

1957 Fairlane 500 Sunliner Convertible

INTRODUCTION

For '63, the Fairlane's front end was deliberately styled to convey a family relationship with the full-size Galaxie.

With all these new products—not to mention the enormously popular Mustang, which started the "pony-car" class—Ford didn't get around to re-engineering its big cars until the '65 model year. Styling became more angular and a bit more formal, though two-door hardtops were still available with the neat, semi-fastback roofline introduced on the 1963½ Galaxie 500 and 500XL models. The simple front end was marked by a bowed-out grille composed of plain horizontal bars. The customary quad headlamps were now arranged vertically instead of horizontally. Bodyside sheetmetal was more rounded, marked by a rather busy array of character lines. A minor facelift for '66 was followed by a heavily revised structure for '67. It featured more pronounced coke-bottle fender contours of the sort GM had popularized two or three years earlier, plus a full fastback roof on the appropriate models and a more imposing frontal treatment. For 1968, the top-of-the-line LTD series, which had replaced the Galaxie 500 in 1965 as the most luxurious big Ford, acquired a hidden-headlamp grille adorned with slim horizontal rectangles and split down the middle. Sheetmetal was again reworked, but retained the visual mass that equated with luxury in the minds of '60s car buyers.

After a decade on a 119-inch wheelbase, the big Ford moved up to a 121-inch chassis for 1969, and the bodyshell changed once more. Styling features included ventless front door glass (in line with the general trend toward flow-through interior ventilation systems in the late '60s), a prominent bulge in the grille and forward hood section, and pronounced tucking under of the rocker panels. LTDs retained hidden headlamps, a styling trick seen as early as the '30s, and which enjoyed a resurgence in the '60s on cars like the Buick Riviera and Cadillac Eldorado. The 1970 full-size Fords were altered only in detail. A holdover from earlier days was the XL (formerly Galaxie 500XL) series, offering

1960 Fairlane 500 4-door sedan

1963½ Galaxie 500XL fastback hardtop coupe

1965 Galaxie 500XL convertible

1967 Galaxie 500XL convertible

1970 XL convertible

1979 LTD Landau 4-door sedan

the sportiness of a bucket-seat interior in a full-size package.

For 1971, a major facelift was instituted. Headlamps were exposed once more, and grilles sprouted a Pontiac-like central beak. Wipers disappeared under the hood's trailing edge, another styling fad popular at the time. Convertibles were beginning to disappear from Detroit, a sign of lagging sales and the industry's concern over reports that the government would enact standards for rollover crash protection. Ford issued its last full-size ragtop for 1972.

Though inner body structure was left alone for 1973, the big Fords were treated to a major reskinning that gave them a totally new look. Rounded forms were becoming passé by now, so fenderlines were straightened and window shapes became more upright and formal. Grilles were now very Lincoln-like, three-element affairs with a broad, slightly protruding center and front fenders extended to carry large, vertical parking lamps. Bumpers became deeper and more prominent—as they had to be to meet the government's new 5-mph impact survivability rule. The '74s used the same themes with only changes in grille inserts to provide model year identification.

By the time the big '75 Fords were announced the country had been through its first fuel shortage, enduring long gas lines and eye-popping fuel price increases. Big-car sales, which had fallen off greatly, began to recover as supplies improved again, but the market was clearly beginning to move away from the truly large size class that had sprung up in the fuel-plentiful '60s. Ford changed its big-car bodyshell once again. Pillarless hardtops disappeared in favor of pillared styles, and the Galaxie name vanished. Two-door coupes featured the much-chided opera windows in the rear quarter roof area and little vertical glass panes in the B-pillar. A large rectangular grille with prominent chrome top band or header was flanked by horizontally disposed headlamps, concealed on topline LTD Landau models. Fenders still jutted forward to carry the parking lamps. This basic look would carry through 1978 with only detail revisions. This makes identifying model years among the big Fords of the mid-'70s a real challenge for the car spotter.

Two years after GM downsized its largest cars, Ford followed suit. The LTD line for 1979 rode a 7-inch shorter wheelbase, yet because of the new body's boxier, higher proportions there was little loss of interior space. There were now two series, LTD and LTD Landau. Both had broader eggcrate grilles and fender-mounted side marker lights. A change in government rules now permitted use of square or retangular headlamps, and these appeared on a big Ford for the first time. Befitting its higher status, the Landau had four of them (the regular LTD made do with two larger units) mounted above wide combination turn signal/parking light units. A chrome bar at the top of the grille carried the Ford name. The raised central hood section of prior years was de-emphasized to heighten the illusion of width on the narrower body.

As you can see from all this, a lot of styling changes have been made over the years—and we've only briefly described just one model line! Of course, dedicated car spotters take pride in being able to name the make, model year, and series of any car they see, and to do so almost at a glance. But human memory being what it is, it never hurts to have an authoritative reference, especially when it comes to settling friendly arguments. That's why the editors of CONSUMER GUIDE® have assembled this *Encyclopedia*. It is, we believe, the first book to present both photos and drawings that enable you to identify series or model lines in any model year for every major U.S. make over a 40-year period.

There is little we need to tell you about how to use the *Car Spotter's Encyclopedia,* but a few words on how the book was prepared may be helpful. First, the book is organized alphabetically by make and by model year within each make. The marques surveyed are the same as those in the *Encyclopedia of American Cars 1940-70* (by Richard M. Langworth and the editors of CONSUMER GUIDE®). In a few cases, we have deviated from those listings for convenience. Thus, Imperial, although officially a separate make after 1954, is combined with parent Chrysler. Similarly, Clipper, a distinct marque for 1956 only, is shown with Packard. Lincoln has used the Continental name on many cars over the years, sometimes for a Lincoln model, at other times as a distinct non-Lincoln marque. Again for convenience, these two nameplates are combined under Lincoln. The tiny British-built Metropolitan of the '50s and early '60s is included here because it was ostensibly a Nash product. It is shown in the Nash section even though some Mets were given Hudson badges and sold through Hudson dealers following the 1954 merger that produced American Motors. Also note that the American Motors section covers only those models bearing AMC emblems. The Rambler marque is treated the same way. Because of its special character and the high enthusiast interest it generates, Corvette is broken out separately from other Chevrolet models. The same holds true for those very special Mustangs created by Carroll Shelby and listed separately from Ford.

For each model year, you'll find detailed line drawings prepared by professional artists showing the car's frontal styling, including hood, grille, and the forward portion of the front fenders. The drawings are placed at the top of the page, and are supported by representative photographs displayed below. Because of space limitations and, in some cases, the great difficulty of locating a suitable number of photos, it was not possible for us to show a picture of every series or model line for each year. However, we have tried to cover major styling variations in the photos as much as possible.

Readers should note that we have deliberately omitted an identifying emblem or nameplate in some drawings where this was the only difference between models or series. This conserves space by allowing one drawing to represent multiple variations. Thus, there was no need to run separate drawings to cover

INTRODUCTION

the four full-size 1961 Pontiac lines. Instead, a single drawing suffices for Catalina, Ventura, Star Chief, and Bonneville. Of course, more substantial differences are handled by separate drawings, as in the case of early-'60s Chryslers, where each series had its own individual grille treatment.

In a few cases, there are virtually no appearance differences from one model year to the next—Avanti II is an example. In such cases, single drawings are used to cover multiple model years as appropriate.

And that just about covers it. Now all you have to do is to look through the thousands of illustrations here and become familiar with the styling points that distinguish U.S. cars between 1940 and 1980 by make, model, and year. Do that, and pretty soon you'll be able to impress your friends as an expert car spotter.

ALLSTATE

1952 DeLuxe 2-door sedan

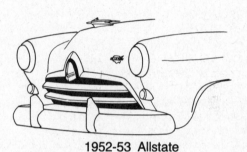

1952-53 Allstate

AMERICAN BANTAM

1940 Boulevard Delivery

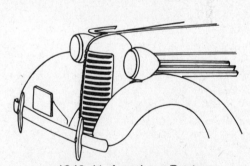

1940-41 American Bantam

1940 roadster

1940 4-passenger speedster

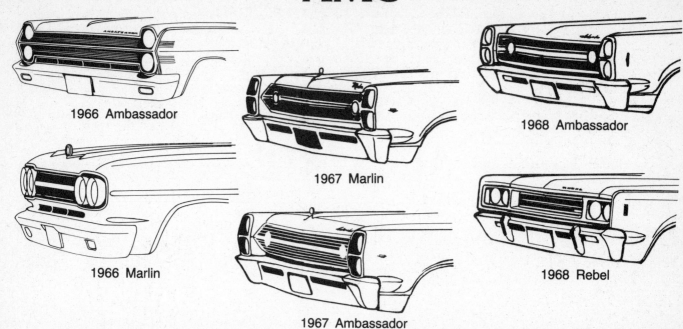

1966 Ambassador

1967 Marlin

1968 Ambassador

1966 Marlin

1967 Ambassador

1968 Rebel

1966 Ambassador 880 2-door sedan

1967 Ambassador DPL hardtop coupe

1967 Marlin fastback hardtop coupe

1968 Ambassador SST 4-door sedan

1967 Marlin fastback hardtop coupe

1968 Ambassador SST hardtop coupe

AMC

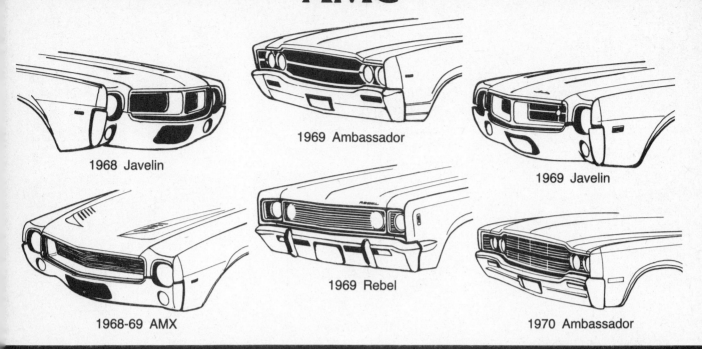

1968 Javelin

1969 Ambassador

1969 Javelin

1968-69 AMX

1969 Rebel

1970 Ambassador

1968 Rebel SST convertible

1968 Javelin SST hardtop coupe

1968 AMX 2-seat fastback coupe

1969 Ambassador SST 4-door sedan

1969 Rebel hardtop coupe

1969 Javelin hardtop coupe

AMC

1970 Rebel

1970-73 Gremlin

1970 AMX

1970 Hornet

1970 Javelin

1971 Ambassador

1970 Rebel SST hardtop coupe

1970 Hornet 2-door sedan

1970 Gremlin 2-door sedan

1971 Javelin AMX hardtop coupe

1971 Matador wagon

1971 Hornet Sportabout wagon

AMC

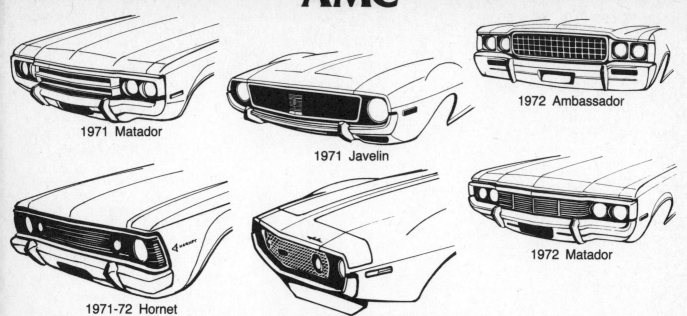

1971 Matador

1971 Javelin

1972 Ambassador

1971-72 Hornet

1971 Javelin AMX

1972 Matador

1971 Gremlin 2-door sedan

1972 Ambassador Brougham wagon

1972 Matador hardtop coupe

1972 Hornet SST 4-door sedan

1972 Gremlin X 2-door sedan

1973 Ambassador Brougham hardtop coupe

AMC

1972 Javelin

1973 Ambassador

1973 Hornet

1972-74 Javelin AMX

1973 Matador

1973-74 Javelin

1973 Matador hardtop coupe

1973 Hornet hatchback coupe

1973 Javelin SST Cardin hardtop coupe

1973 Gremlin X "Levi's" 2-door sedan

1974 Ambassador Brougham 4-door sedan

1974 Matador 4-door sedan

1974 Ambassador

1974 Matador sedan

1974 Hornet

1974-75 Matador coupe

1974-75 Gremlin

1975-77 Matador sedan

1974 Matador X fastback coupe

1974 Hornet 2-door sedan

1974 Gremlin X "Levi's" 2-door sedan

1974 Javelin AMX hardtop coupe

1975 Matador X fastback coupe

1975 Hornet D/L 4-door sedan

1975-77 Hornet

1976-77 Matador coupe

1977-78 Gremlin

1975-77 Pacer

1976 Gremlin

1977 Hornet AMX

1975 Pacer D/L 3-door sedan

1976 Gremlin 2-door sedan

1976 Matador Brougham 4-door sedan

1976 Matador Barcelona fastback coupe

1977 Hornet AMX hatchback coupe

1977 Matador Barcelona fastback coupe

AMC

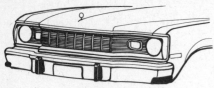

1978 Matador

1978 AMX

1979-80 Pacer

1978 Pacer

1978 Concord

1979 AMX

1977 Matador wagon

1978 Matador Barcelona 4-door sedan

1977 Gremlin X 2-door sedan

1978 Pacer D/L 3-door sedan

1977 Pacer D/L 3-door wagon

1978 Concord D/L 2-door sedan

AMC

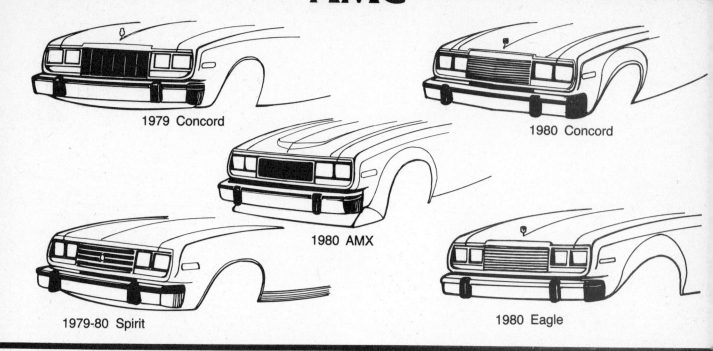

1979 Concord

1980 Concord

1980 AMX

1979-80 Spirit

1980 Eagle

1979 Concord DL hatchback coupe

1980 Spirit DL Liftback coupe

1979 Spirit Limited 2-door sedan

1980 Eagle 2-door sedan

1979 AMX Liftback coupe

1980 Concord DL 2-door sedan

AVANTI II

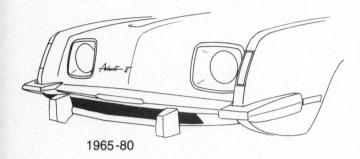

1965-80

Leo Newman and Nathan Altman, partners in a Studebaker dealership, bought the name and production rights to the Avanti after Studebaker moved to Canada in 1963. The Avanti II has been built since 1965 in a former Studebaker factory in South Bend, Ind., and has changed little in appearance except to meet federal safety rules. The handbuilt Avanti II can be tailored to a buyer's personal desires.

1980 sport coupe

1980 sport coupe

1980 sport coupe

BUICK

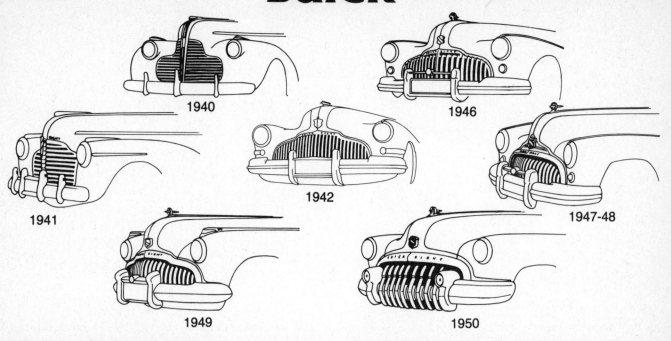

1940

1946

1941

1942

1947-48

1949

1950

1940 Series 60 Century sport coupe

1941 Series 70 Roadmaster convertible phaeton

1940 Series 80 Limited Streamlined formal sedan

1941 Series 50 Super convertible phaeton

1941 Series 90 Limited 8-passenger sedan

1941 Series 60 Century business coupe

BUICK

1951

1952

1953

1954

1955

1956

1957

1958

1942 Series 40B Special 4-door sedan

1946 Series 40 Special sedanet

1942 Series 70 Roadmaster convertible coupe

1947 Series 50 Super 4-door sedan

1946 Series 70 Roadmaster sedanet

1948 Series 70 Roadmaster 4-door sedan

BUICK

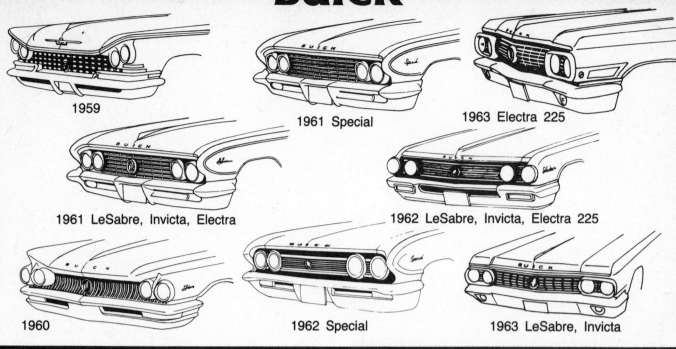

1959

1961 Special

1963 Electra 225

1961 LeSabre, Invicta, Electra

1962 LeSabre, Invicta, Electra 225

1960

1962 Special

1963 LeSabre, Invicta

1949 Series 70 Roadmaster Riviera hardtop coupe

1950 Series 40 Special fastback sedan

1949 Series 50 Super sedanet

1951 Series 50 Super convertible

1950 Series 50 Super Riviera hardtop coupe

1951 Series 50 Super sedanet

BUICK

1963 Wildcat

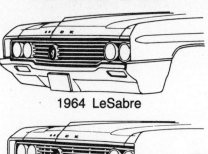

1964 LeSabre

1964 Electra 225

1964 Wildcat

1963 Special

1963 Riviera

1964 Riviera

1951 Series 40 Special sport coupe

1954 Series 70 Roadmaster convertible

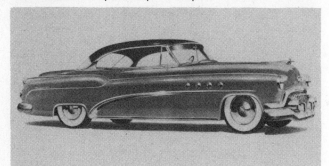

1952 Series 70 Roadmaster Riviera hardtop coupe

1954 Series 60 Century 4-door sedan

1953 Series 70 Roadmaster Riviera 4-door sedan

1955 Series 60 Century convertible

BUICK

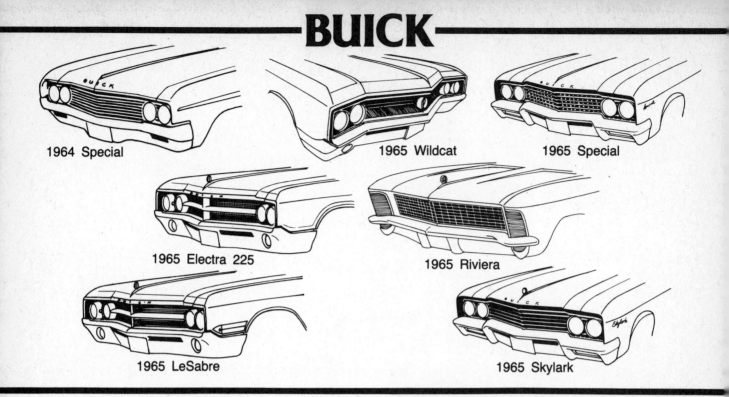

1964 Special   1965 Wildcat   1965 Special

1965 Electra 225   1965 Riviera

1965 LeSabre   1965 Skylark

1955 Series 60 Century Riviera hardtop coupe

1955 Series 40 Special 4-door sedan

1956 Series 60 Century Riviera hardtop coupe

1956 Series 70 Roadmaster Riviera hardtop sedan

1957 Series 60 Century Caballero hardtop wagon

1957 Series 60 Century convertible

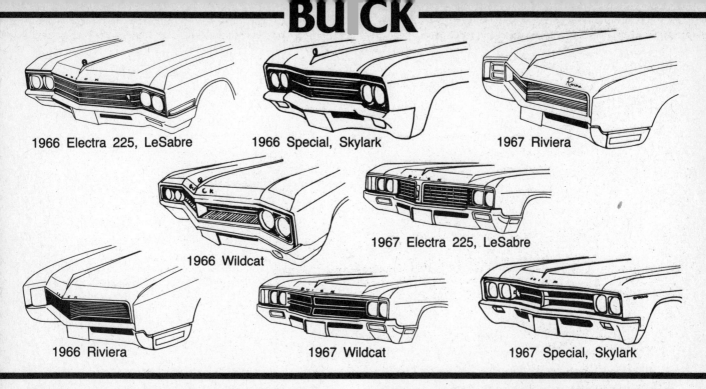

1966 Electra 225, LeSabre   1966 Special, Skylark   1967 Riviera

1966 Wildcat

1967 Electra 225, LeSabre

1966 Riviera   1967 Wildcat   1967 Special, Skylark

1957 Series 70 Roadmaster convertible

1958 Series 700 Limited hardtop coupe

1958 Series 50 Super hardtop sedan

1958 Series 40 Special 2-door sedan

1959 Invicta 4-door sedan

1959 LeSabre hardtop sedan

BUICK

1968 Electra 225

1968 Riviera

1969 Electra 225

1968 LeSabre

1969 LeSabre

1968 Wildcat

1968 Skylark, Special

1969 Wildcat

1960 Electra 225 Riviera hardtop sedan

1962 Electra 225 hardtop coupe

1961 Invicta hardtop coupe

1962 Special convertible

1962 Electra 225 Riviera hardtop sedan

1963 Riviera hardtop coupe

BUICK

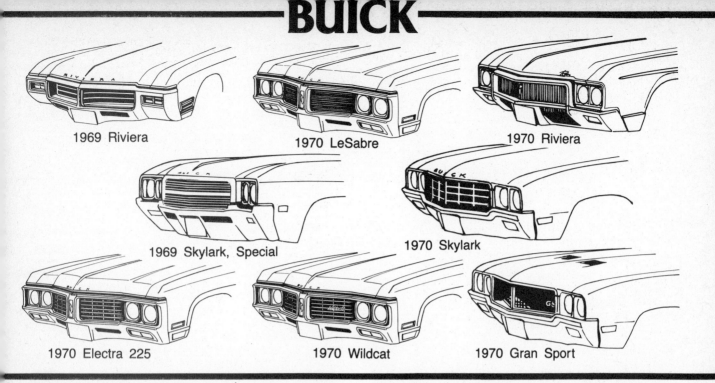

1969 Riviera   1970 LeSabre   1970 Riviera

1969 Skylark, Special   1970 Skylark

1970 Electra 225   1970 Wildcat   1970 Gran Sport

1964 Riviera hardtop coupe

1964 Wildcat hardtop coupe

1965 Electra 225 Custom convertible

1965 LeSabre Custom hardtop coupe

1965 Skylark Custom 4-door sedan

1966 Special Deluxe 4-door sedan

BUICK

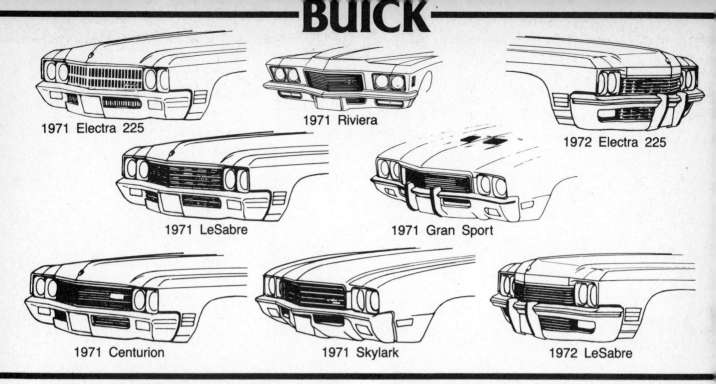

1971 Electra 225   1971 Riviera   1972 Electra 225

1971 LeSabre   1971 Gran Sport

1971 Centurion   1971 Skylark   1972 LeSabre

1967 Riviera GS hardtop coupe

1967 Special Deluxe 4-door sedan

1968 Riviera hardtop coupe

1968 Electra 225 Custom hardtop coupe

1968 LeSabre Custom convertible

1968 Skylark Custom hardtop coupe

BUICK

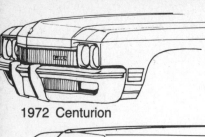

1972 Centurion

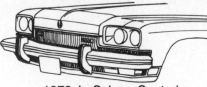

1973 LeSabre, Centurion

1973 Century

1972 Riviera

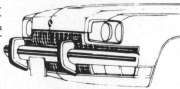

1973 Electra 225

1973 Riviera

1972 Skylark

1973 Century Regal

1973 Apollo

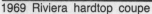

1969 Riviera hardtop coupe

1969 LeSabre hardtop sedan

1969 Electra 225 Custom hardtop coupe

1969 GS400 hardtop coupe

1969 Wildcat hardtop coupe

1969 SportWagon

BUICK

1974 Electra 225

1974 Century Regal

1975 Electra 225

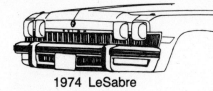
1974 LeSabre

1974 Century

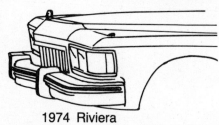
1974 Riviera

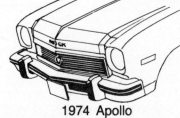
1974 Apollo

1975 LeSabre

1970 Riviera hardtop coupe

1970 GS455 hardtop coupe

1970 Wildcat Custom convertible

1970 Estate Wagon

1970 LeSabre hardtop sedan

1971 Centurion hardtop coupe

BUICK

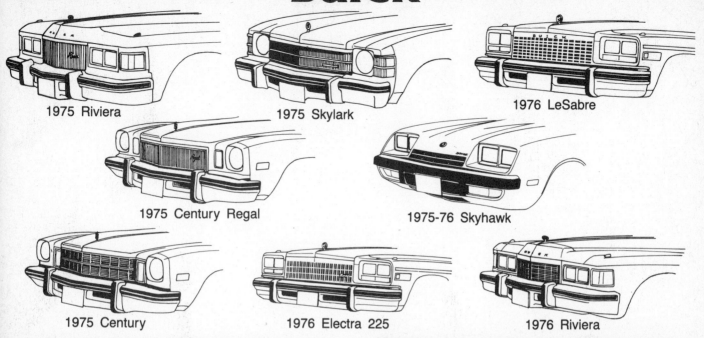

1975 Riviera   1975 Skylark   1976 LeSabre

1975 Century Regal   1975-76 Skyhawk

1975 Century   1976 Electra 225   1976 Riviera

1971 Riviera GS hardtop coupe

1972 Estate Wagon

1972 Riviera hardtop coupe

1972 Riviera GS hardtop coupe

1972 Electra 225 Limited hardtop sedan

1973 LeSabre Custom hardtop sedan

BUICK

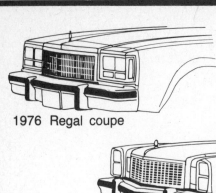

1976 Regal coupe

1976 Skylark

1977 Riviera

1976 Century, Regal sedans

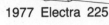

1977 Electra 225

1976 Century coupes

1977 LeSabre

1977 Regal coupe

1973 Regal Colonnade hardtop coupe

1974 Century Luxus Colonnade hardtop coupe

1973 Apollo 2-door sedan

1975 Century Special Colonnade hardtop coupe

1974 Riviera coupe

1975 Apollo hatchback sedan

BUICK

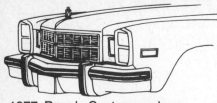
1977 Regal, Century sedans

1977-78 Skyhawk

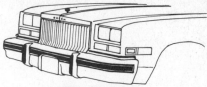
1978 Riviera

1977 Century coupe

1978 Electra 225

1977 Skylark

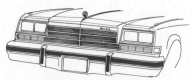
1978 LeSabre

1978 Regal

1975 Skyhawk hatchback coupe

1976 Century Special coupe

1976 LeSabre Custom hardtop sedan

1976 Skylark 4-door sedan

1976 Century Custom coupe

1977 Riviera coupe

BUICK

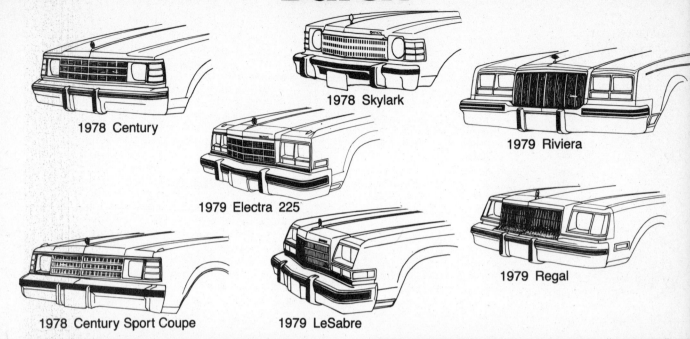

1978 Century

1978 Skylark

1979 Riviera

1979 Electra 225

1978 Century Sport Coupe

1979 LeSabre

1979 Regal

1977 Electra Limited coupe

1978 LeSabre Sport Coupe

1977 LeSabre Custom coupe

1978 Estate Wagon

1977 Regal coupe

1978 Regal Sport Coupe

BUICK

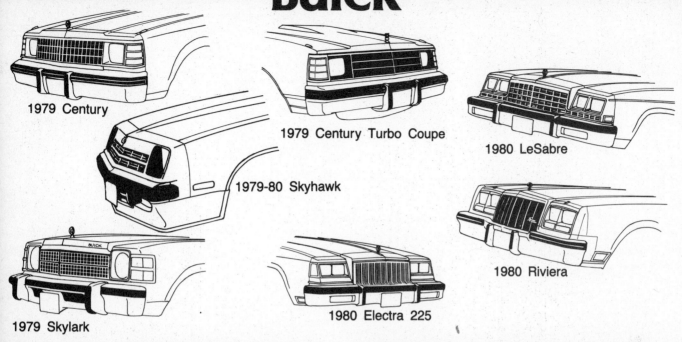

1979 Century

1979 Century Turbo Coupe

1980 LeSabre

1979-80 Skyhawk

1980 Riviera

1979 Skylark

1980 Electra 225

1978 Century Custom 4-door sedan

1979 Electra Limited coupe

1978 Century Special coupe

1979 Riviera S-Type coupe

1978 Buick Skyhawk hatchback coupe

1979 Century Limited 4-door sedan

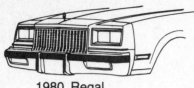
1980 Regal

1980 Skylark

1980 Century Turbo Coupe

1980 Century

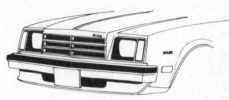
1980 Skylark Sport

1980 Electra Limited coupe

1980 Century Estate Wagon

1980 Riviera S-Type coupe

1980 Skylark Sport Coupe

1980 Regal Somerset coupe

1980 Skylark Limited 4-door sedan

CADILLAC

1940 Series 60 Special, 62, 72, 75

1940 Sixteen

1941

1942-45

1940 Sixteen Town Sedan

1940 Fleetwood Series 75 convertible coupe

1940 Fleetwood Series 75 town car

1940 Fleetwood Series 60 Special 4-door sedan

1941 Series 67 Touring Sedan

1941 Series 62 convertible coupe

1942 Fleetwood Series 60 Special 4-door sedan

1942 Fleetwood Series 60 Special 4-door sedan

CADILLAC

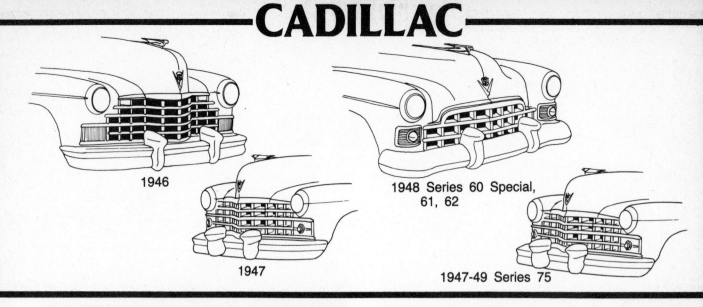

1946

1947

1948 Series 60 Special, 61, 62

1947-49 Series 75

1942 Series 61 club coupe

1946 Fleetwood Series 60 Special 4-door sedan

1947 Series 61 4-door sedan

1947 Series 62 convertible

1948 Series 62 4-door sedan

1949 Series 62 Coupe de Ville hardtop coupe

Fleetwood Series 75 limousine proposed for 1949

1950 Fleetwood Series 60 Special 4-door sedan

CADILLAC

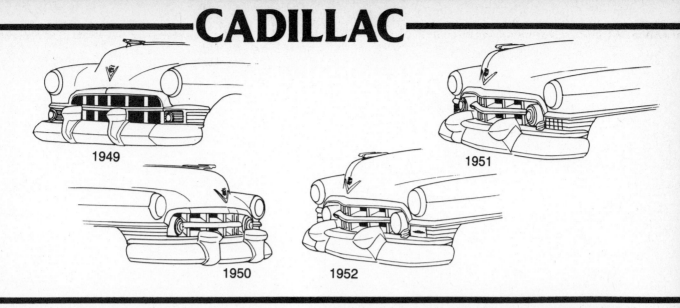

1949

1951

1950

1952

1950 Series 61 4-door sedan

1951 Series 62 convertible

1951 Series 62 Coupe de Ville hardtop coupe

1952 Fleetwood Series 60 Special 4-door sedan

1952 Series 62 Coupe de Ville hardtop coupe

1953 Fleetwood Series 75 Imperial sedan

1953 Series 62 Coupe de Ville hardtop coupe

1953 Series 62 convertible

CADILLAC

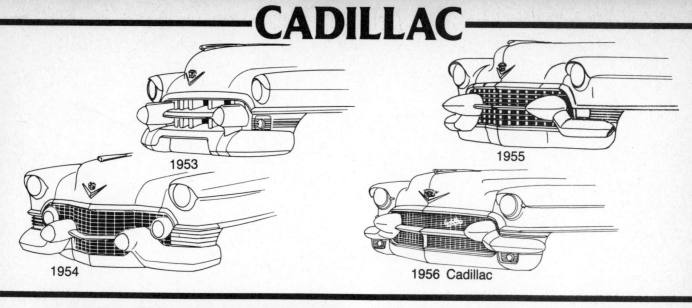

1953

1955

1954

1956 Cadillac

1953 Fleetwood Series 60 Special 4-door sedan

1954 Fleetwood Series 75 limousine

1954 Series 62 hardtop coupe

1954 Series 62 convertible

1955 Fleetwood Series 75 8-passenger sedan

1955 Series 62 convertible

1955 Series 62 Coupe de Ville hardtop coupe

1957 Series 70 Eldorado Brougham hardtop sedan

CADILLAC

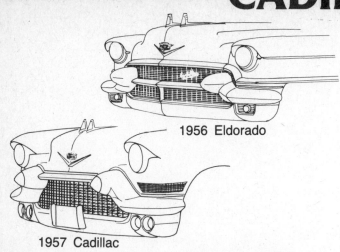

1956 Eldorado

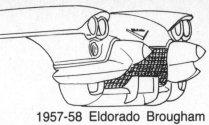

1957-58 Eldorado Brougham

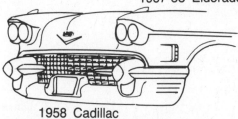

1957 Cadillac

1958 Cadillac

1957 Fleetwood Series 60 Special hardtop sedan

1957 Series 62 hardtop coupe

1957 Series 62 Sedan de Ville hardtop sedan

1958 Series 70 Eldorado Brougham hardtop sedan

1957 Series 62 convertible

1958 Series 62 Eldorado Biarritz convertible

1957 Series 62 Eldorado Seville hardtop coupe

1958 Series 62 hardtop coupe

CADILLAC

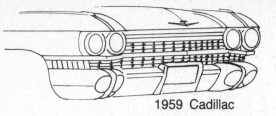

1959 Cadillac

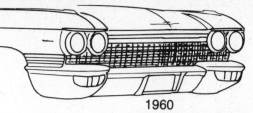

1960

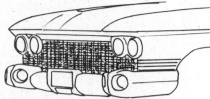

1959 Eldorado Brougham

1961

1958 Series 62 Eldorado Seville hardtop coupe

1959 Series 62 6-window hardtop sedan

1959 Fleetwood Series 75 limousine

1960 Fleetwood Series 60 Special hardtop sedan

1959 Eldorado Biarritz convertible

1960 Series 62 hardtop coupe

1959 Eldorado Seville hardtop coupe

1961 Series 62 hardtop coupe

CADILLAC

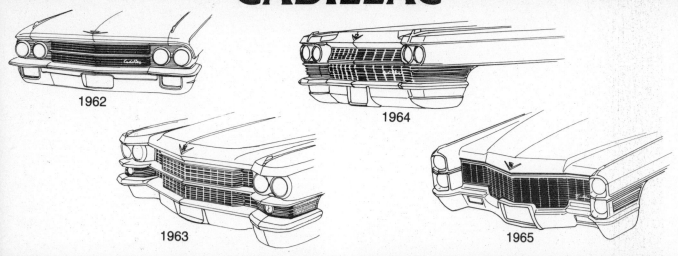

1962

1964

1963

1965

1962 Sedan de Ville 6-window hardtop sedan

1964 Sedan de Ville 4-window hardtop sedan

1962 Series 62 convertible

1964 Series 62 hardtop coupe

1963 Sedan de Ville 4-window hardtop sedan

1965 Fleetwood Eldorado convertible

1964 Fleetwood Eldorado Biarritz convertible

1965 Fleetwood Sixty Special sedan

CADILLAC

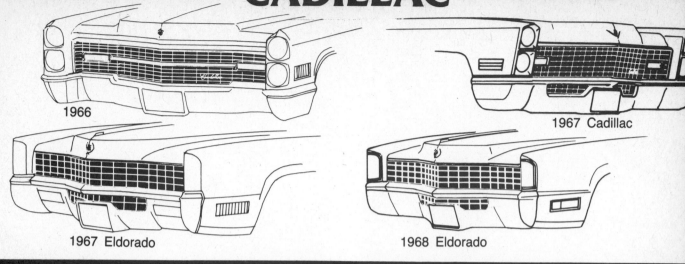

1966

1967 Cadillac

1967 Eldorado

1968 Eldorado

1965 Calais 4-door sedan

1966 Calais hardtop coupe

1965 Calais hardtop coupe

1967 Sixty Special Fleetwood Brougham sedan

1966 Fleetwood Seventy-Five sedan

1967 Fleetwood Eldorado hardtop coupe

1966 Coupe de Ville hardtop coupe

1967 Coupe de Ville hardtop coupe

CADILLAC

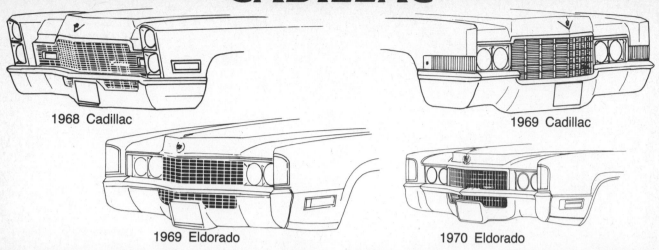

1968 Cadillac   1969 Cadillac

1969 Eldorado   1970 Eldorado

1968 De Ville convertible

1969 Fleetwood Eldorado hardtop coupe

1968 Fleetwood Eldorado hardtop coupe

1969 Sedan de Ville hardtop sedan

1968 Sedan de Ville hardtop sedan

1970 De Ville convertible

1969 Sixty Special Fleetwood Brougham sedan

1970 Coupe de Ville hardtop coupe

CADILLAC

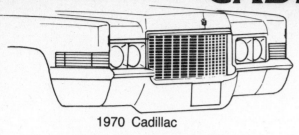

1970 Cadillac

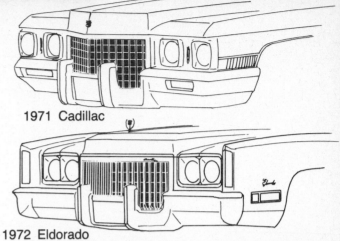

1971 Cadillac

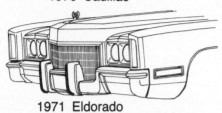

1971 Eldorado

1972 Eldorado

1970 Sedan de Ville hardtop sedan

1972 Fleetwood Sixty Special Brougham sedan

1970 Sedan de Ville hardtop sedan

1972 Fleetwood Eldorado coupe

1971 Fleetwood Sixty Special Brougham sedan

1972 Sedan de Ville hardtop sedan

1971 Fleetwood Eldorado convertible

1973 Fleetwood Sixty Special Brougham sedan

CADILLAC

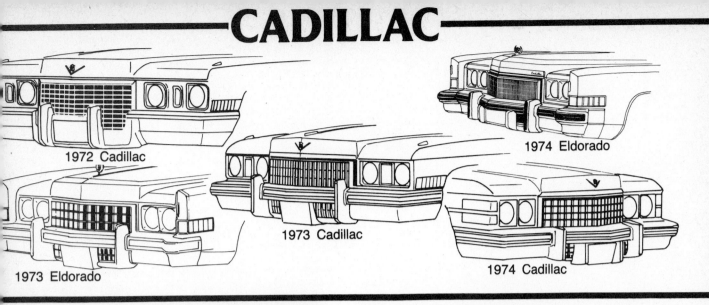

1972 Cadillac

1974 Eldorado

1973 Cadillac

1974 Cadillac

1973 Eldorado

1973 Fleetwood Eldorado coupe

1975 Sedan de Ville hardtop sedan

1973 Fleetwood Eldorado convertible

1975 Fleetwood Eldorado coupe

1973 Sedan de Ville hardtop sedan

1975 Coupe de Ville coupe

1974 Fleetwood Sixty Special Brougham sedan

1976 Fleetwood Brougham sedan

CADILLAC

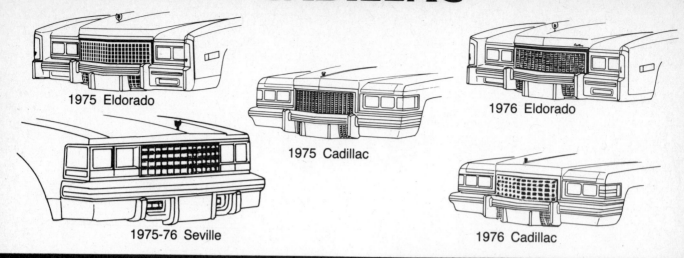

1975 Eldorado

1975 Cadillac

1976 Eldorado

1975-76 Seville

1976 Cadillac

1976 Fleetwood Eldorado convertible

1976 Seville sedan

1976 Calais hardtop sedan

1977 Sedan de Ville sedan

1977 Coupe de Ville coupe

1977 Fleetwood Eldorado coupe

1977 Seville Elegante (show car)

1978 Fleetwood Brougham sedan

CADILLAC

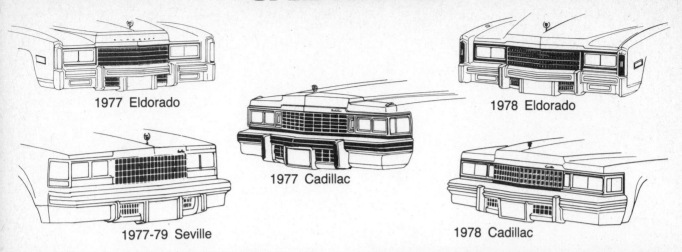

1977 Eldorado   1977 Cadillac   1978 Eldorado

1977-79 Seville   1978 Cadillac

1978 Fleetwood Eldorado coupe

1978 Seville Elegante sedan

1978 Fleetwood Eldorado Custom Biarritz Classic

1979 Coupe de Ville coupe

1978 Coupe de Ville coupe

1979 Eldorado Biarritz coupe

1978 Sedan de Ville sedan

1979 Sedan de Ville sedan

CADILLAC

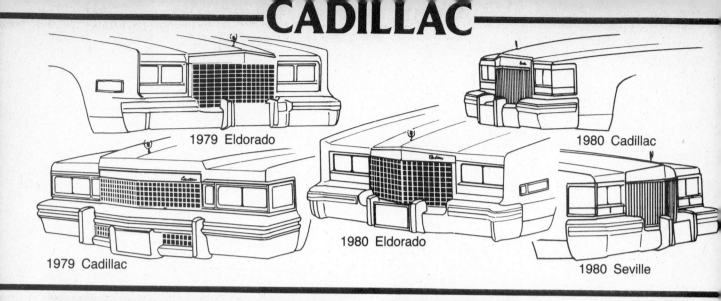

1979 Eldorado

1980 Cadillac

1980 Eldorado

1979 Cadillac

1980 Seville

1979 Eldorado coupe

1980 Eldorado coupe

1979 Eldorado coupe

1980 Eldorado Biarritz coupe

1979 De Ville Special Edition "Phaeton" coupe

1980 Coupe de Ville coupe

1980 Fleetwood Brougham sedan

1980 Seville Elegante sedan

52

CHECKER

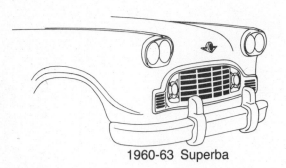

1960-63 Superba

1961-80 Marathon

1966 Marathon limousine

1966 Marathon Deluxe sedan

1967 Marathon sedan

Checker began marketing passenger cars in 1960 when it offered the Superba. The Marathon, famed as the workhorse of taxicab fleets, has changed little since it was introduced in 1961. Appearance changes to the Marathon have mainly been in response to federal safety requirements such as side marker lights and energy-absorbing bumpers. Checker Motors Corporation was organized in 1922.

1979 Marathon sedan

CHEVROLET

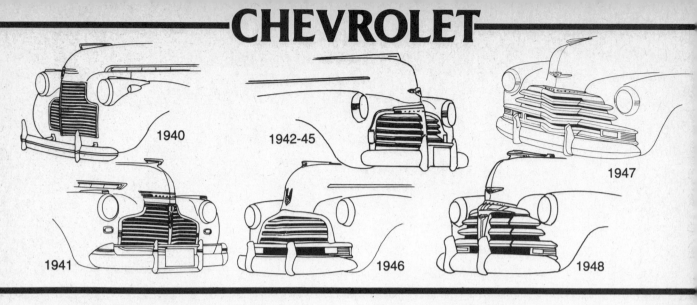

1940 1942-45 1947 1941 1946 1948

1940 Master Deluxe Sport Sedan

1941 Special DeLuxe Town Sedan

1942 Special DeLuxe Fleetmaster 5-passenger coupe

1946 Stylemaster Sport Sedan

1941 Special DeLuxe Sport Sedan

1947 Fleetmaster Sport Sedan

1947 Fleetmaster wagon

CHEVROLET

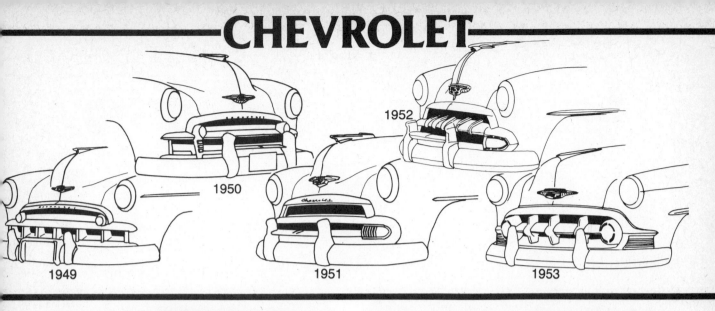

1950

1952

1949

1951

1953

1948 Fleetline Aerosedan

1949 Styleline DeLuxe Sport Sedan

1949 Styleline DeLuxe wood-body wagon

1950 Styleline DeLuxe Sport Sedan

1951 Styleline DeLuxe Bel Air hardtop coupe

1951 Styleline DeLuxe 4-door sedan

1952 Styleline DeLuxe 4-door sedan

1952 Styleline DeLuxe sport coupe

CHEVROLET

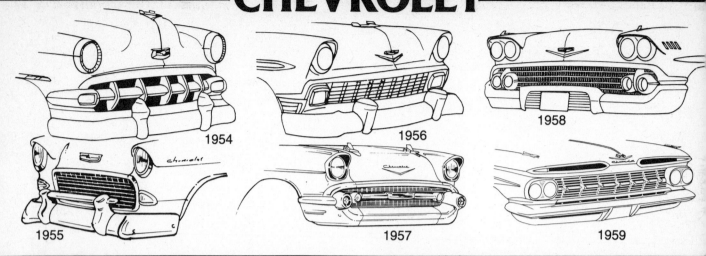

1954

1956

1958

1955

1957

1959

1953 Two-Ten 4-door sedan

1953 Bel Air 4-door sedan

1953 Bel Air convertible

1954 Bel Air 4-door sedan

1955 Two-Ten Sport Coupe

1955 Bel Air convertible

1955 Bel Air Nomad hardtop wagon

1956 Bel Air Sport Sedan

CHEVROLET

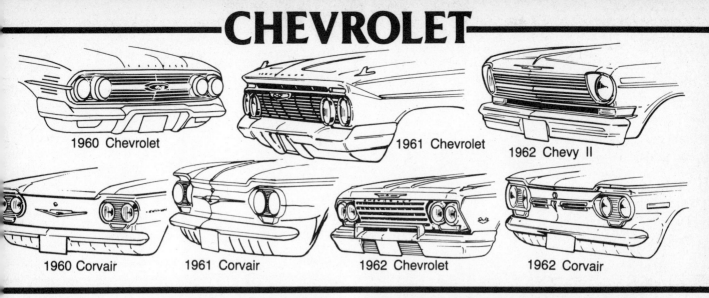

1960 Chevrolet   1961 Chevrolet   1962 Chevy II

1960 Corvair   1961 Corvair   1962 Chevrolet   1962 Corvair

1956 Bel Air Nomad hardtop wagon

1957 Bel Air Nomad hardtop wagon

1957 Two-Ten 4-door sedan

1957 Bel Air convertible

1957 Bel Air 4-door sedan

1958 Bel Air Impala Sport Coupe

1957 One-Fifty utility sedan

1958 Bel Air Impala convertible

CHEVROLET

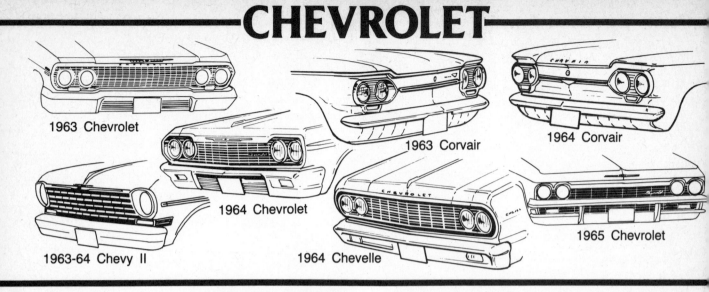

1963 Chevrolet

1963 Corvair

1964 Corvair

1964 Chevrolet

1963-64 Chevy II

1964 Chevelle

1965 Chevrolet

1959 Impala 4-door sedan

1959 Biscayne 2-door sedan

1960 Impala Sport Sedan

1960 Impala convertible

1960 Corvair 500 sedan

1961 Impala 2-door sedan

1961 Impala Sport Sedan

1961 Corvair 700 Lakewood wagon

CHEVROLET

1965 Chevelle

1965 Corvair

1966 Chevelle

1965 Chevy II

1966 Chevrolet

1966 Chevy II

1962 Impala Sport Coupe

1962 Bel Air 4-door sedan

1962 Chevy II 300 2-door sedan

1962 Corvair 700 wagon

1963 Impala convertible

1963 Impala Sport Coupe

1963 Chevy II Nova SS Sport Coupe

1963 Corvair Monza Spyder convertible

CHEVROLET

1966-69 Corvair

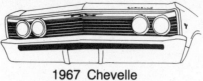

1967 Chevelle

1967 Camaro

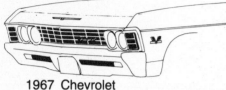

1967 Chevrolet

1967 Chevy II

1968 Chevrolet

1964 Impala convertible

1964 Impala SS Sport Coupe

1964 Chevelle Malibu SS convertible

1964 Chevelle Malibu SS Sport Coupe

1964 Corvair Monza club coupe

1964 Corvair Monza Spyder convertible

1965 Impala SS convertible

1965 Impala Caprice hardtop sedan

Chevelles were available in three series when the model line was introduced in 1964: the base 300, the Malibu, and the Malibu SS. SS models were available with 6-cylinder engines in 1964 and 1965, but came only with the 396-cid V-8 in 1966.

CHEVROLET

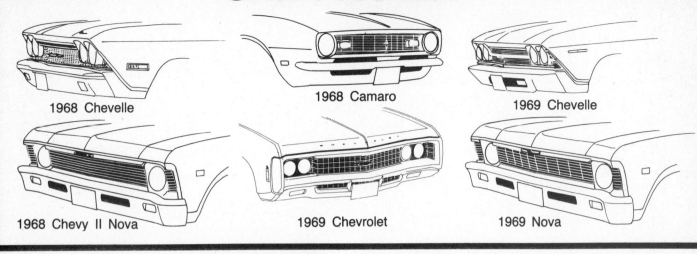

1968 Chevelle   1968 Camaro   1969 Chevelle

1968 Chevy II Nova   1969 Chevrolet   1969 Nova

1965 Impala hardtop coupe

1965 Chevy II Nova SS hardtop coupe

1965 Corvair Corsa hardtop coupe

1965 Corvair Corsa convertible

1966 Impala SS convertible

1966 Caprice hardtop sedan

1966 Chevelle SS396 hardtop coupe

1966 Corvair Corsa hardtop coupe

CHEVROLET

1969 Camaro   1970 Chevelle   1970-72 Nova

1970 Chevrolet   1970 Monte Carlo   1970-71 Camaro

1966 Chevy II Nova SS hardtop coupe

1967 Caprice hardtop sedan

1967 Impala SS convertible

1967 Chevelle Malibu hardtop sedan

1967 Chevelle SS396 hardtop coupe

1967 Camaro hardtop coupe

1967 Camaro SS 350 hardtop coupe

1967 Camaro SS 350 convertible

CHEVROLET

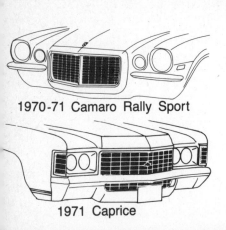

1970-71 Camaro Rally Sport

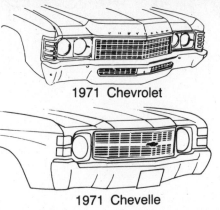

1971 Chevrolet

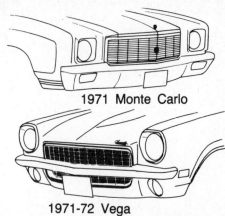

1971 Monte Carlo

1971 Caprice

1971 Chevelle

1971-72 Vega

1967 Chevy II Nova SS hardtop coupe

1967 Corvair Monza hardtop sedan

1968 Caprice hardtop coupe

1968 Impala convertible

1968 Chevelle Malibu 4-door sedan

1968 Chevelle SS396 convertible

1968 Chevelle SS396 hardtop coupe

1968 Camaro hardtop coupe

CHEVROLET

1972 Caprice

1972 Chevelle

1972 Camaro

1972 Chevrolet

1972 Monte Carlo

1972 Camaro Rally Sport

1968 Camaro Rally Sport hardtop coupe (prototype)

1968 Chevy II Nova 4-door sedan

1968 Chevy II Nova SS 2-door sedan

1969 Impala Custom hardtop coupe

1969 Kingswood Estate wagon

1969 Biscayne 2-door sedan

1969 Chevelle Malibu 4-door sedan

1969 Camaro Z-28 hardtop coupe

After restyling the Chevy II series in 1968, Chevrolet renamed it "Nova." The Nova name had been used on top-of-the-line Chevy II models since the series was introduced in 1962. The Nova line was replaced in 1980 by the front-drive Citation.

CHEVROLET

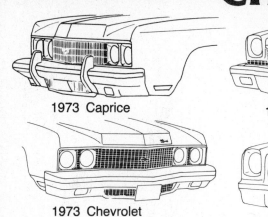

1973 Caprice

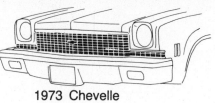

1973 Chevelle

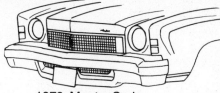

1973 Monte Carlo

1973 Chevrolet

1973 Chevelle Laguna

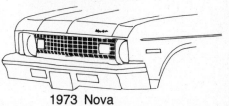

1973 Nova

1969 Camaro Rally Sport convertible

1969 Corvair Monza convertible

1970 Monte Carlo hardtop coupe

1970 Impala Custom hardtop coupe

1970 Kingswood Estate wagon

1970 Chevelle Malibu Sport Sedan

1970 Chevelle SS396 Sport Coupe

1970 Camaro Sport Coupe

CHEVROLET

1973 Camaro

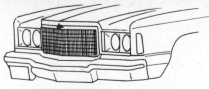
1974 Caprice

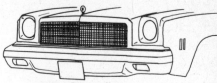
1974 Chevelle

1973 Vega

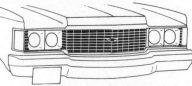
1974 Chevrolet

1974 Chevelle Laguna

1970 Camaro Sport Coupe

1970 Nova 2-door sedan

1971 Caprice hardtop coupe

1971 Chevelle Malibu Sport Coupe

1971 Chevelle SS396 Sport Coupe

1971 Camaro SS Sport Coupe

1971 Camaro Z-28 Sport Coupe

1971 Vega 2300 hatchback coupe

CHEVROLET

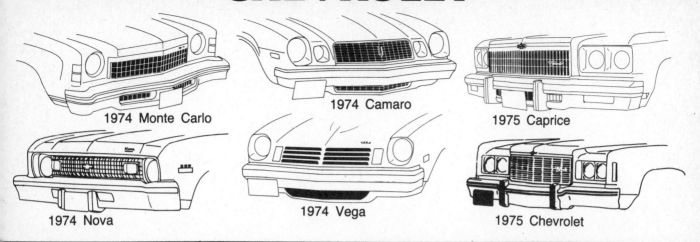

1974 Monte Carlo   1974 Camaro   1975 Caprice

1974 Nova   1974 Vega   1975 Chevrolet

1971 Vega 2300 Kammback wagon

1972 Caprice hardtop sedan

1972 Kingswood Estate wagon

1972 Monte Carlo hardtop coupe

1972 Chevelle Malibu Sport Coupe

1972 Camaro Sport Coupe

1972 Nova Custom 2-door sedan

1973 Caprice hardtop coupe

CHEVROLET

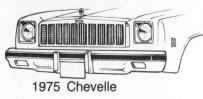
1975 Chevelle

1975 Monte Carlo

1975-77 Camaro

1975 Chevelle Laguna

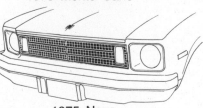
1975 Nova

1975-77 Monza 2+2

1973 Impala Custom hardtop coupe

1973 Monte Carlo coupe

1973 Chevelle Malibu Colonnade hardtop coupe

1973 Chevelle Laguna Colonnade hardtop coupe

1973 Camaro Type LT Sport Coupe

1973 Nova hatchback sedan

1973 Vega hatchback coupe

1974 Caprice coupe

CHEVROLET

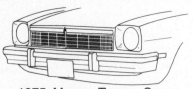
1975 Monza Towne Coupe

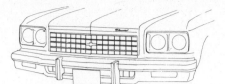
1976 Impala

1976 Chevelle Malibu

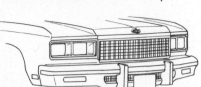
1976 Caprice

1976 Chevelle Malibu Classic

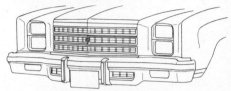
1976 Monte Carlo

1974 Caprice Estate Wagon

1974 Camaro Type LT Sport Coupe

1974 Impala hardtop sedan

1974 Nova Custom 4-door sedan

1974 Monte Carlo coupe

1974 Vega Estate Wagon

1974 Chevelle Laguna S-3 Colonnade hardtop coupe

1975 Caprice Classic hardtop sedan

69

CHEVROLET

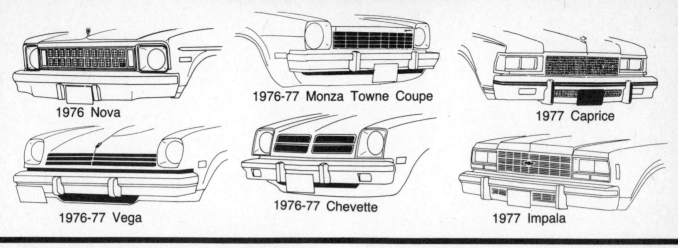

1976 Nova

1976-77 Monza Towne Coupe

1977 Caprice

1976-77 Vega

1976-77 Chevette

1977 Impala

1975 Monte Carlo Landau coupe

1975 Chevelle Malibu Classic coupe

1975 Nova LN coupe

1975 Camaro Type LT Sport Coupe

1975 Vega 2-door sedan

1975 Vega GT Kammback wagon

1975 Monza 2+2 hatchback coupe

1975 Monza Towne Coupe

CHEVROLET

1977 Chevelle Malibu Classic

1977 Monte Carlo

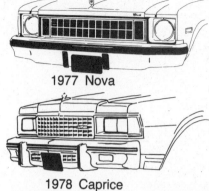
1977 Nova

1977 Concours

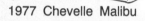
1977 Chevelle Malibu

1978 Caprice

1976 Caprice Classic hardtop sedan

1976 Impala Custom Coupe

1976 Chevelle Malibu Classic Landau coupe

1976 Monte Carlo Landau coupe

1976 Nova Concours hatchback coupe

1976 Chevette Rally 1.6 2-door hatchback sedan

1976 Chevette Woody 2-door hatchback sedan

1977 Caprice Classic 4-door sedan

CHEVROLET

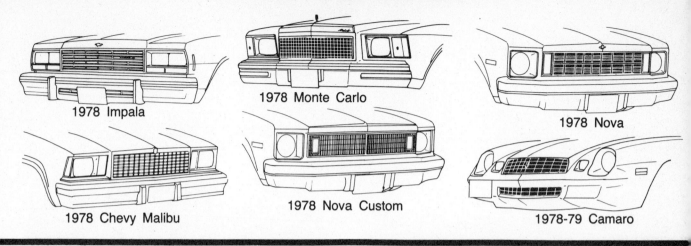

1978 Impala   1978 Monte Carlo   1978 Nova

1978 Chevy Malibu   1978 Nova Custom   1978-79 Camaro

1977 Monte Carlo Landau coupe

1977 Concours 4-door sedan

1977 Camaro Z-28 Sport Coupe

1977 Monza Spyder hatchback coupe

1977 Monza Sport Towne Coupe

1977 Vega GT hatchback coupe

1978 Impala coupe

1978 Monte Carlo coupe

CHEVROLET

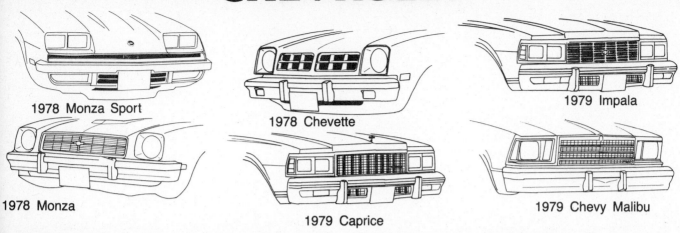

1978 Monza Sport

1978 Chevette

1979 Impala

1978 Monza

1979 Caprice

1979 Chevy Malibu

1978 Malibu Classic Landau coupe

1978 Monza Estate Wagon

1978 Nova Custom 4-door sedan

1978 Chevette 4-door hatchback sedan

1978 Camaro Sport Coupe

1979 Caprice Classic wagon

1978 Monza 2+2 hatchback coupe

1979 Monte Carlo coupe

73

CHEVROLET

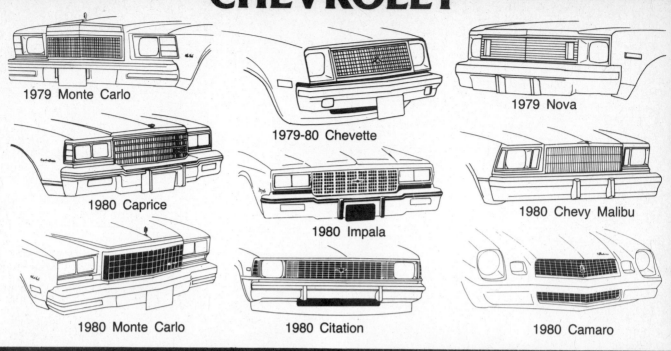

1979 Monte Carlo

1979-80 Chevette

1979 Nova

1980 Caprice

1980 Impala

1980 Chevy Malibu

1980 Monte Carlo

1980 Citation

1980 Camaro

1979 Camaro Z-28 Sport Coupe

1979 Monza Spyder hatchback coupe

1979 Malibu coupe

1980 Impala 4-door sedan

1980 Citation club coupe

1980 Citation X-11 2-door hatchback sedan

CHEVROLET CORVETTE

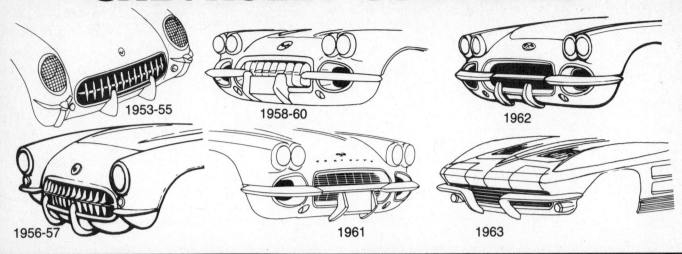

1953-55   1958-60   1962

1956-57   1961   1963

1954 roadster

1955 roadster

1956 convertible with hardtop

1958 convertible with hardtop

1959 convertible

1960 convertible

1962 convertible

1963 Sting Ray coupe

CHEVROLET CORVETTE

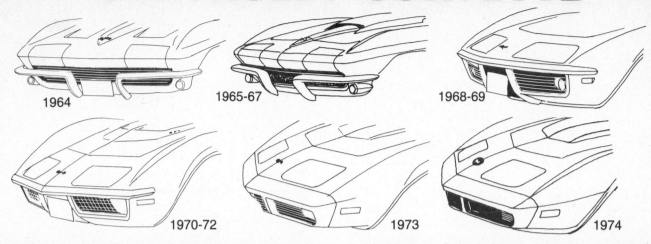

1964   1965-67   1968-69

1970-72   1973   1974

1964 Sting Ray convertible

1965 Sting Ray coupe

1966 Sting Ray coupe

Corvettes were called Sting Rays from
1963 to 1967, but the name was dropped
for 1968. Chevrolet resurrected the name
in 1969, when it became one word: Stingray.

1968 convertible

1969 Stingray coupe

1971 Stingray coupe

1972 Stingray coupe

1972 Stingray coupe

CHEVROLET CORVETTE

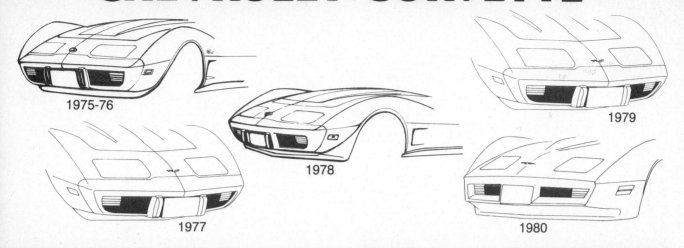

1975-76

1978

1977

1979

1980

1973 Stingray coupe

1974 Stingray coupe

1975 Stingray coupe

1976 Stingray coupe

1978 Silver Anniversary Edition coupe

1978 Pace Car Replica coupe

1979 coupe

1980 coupe

CHRYSLER & IMPERIAL

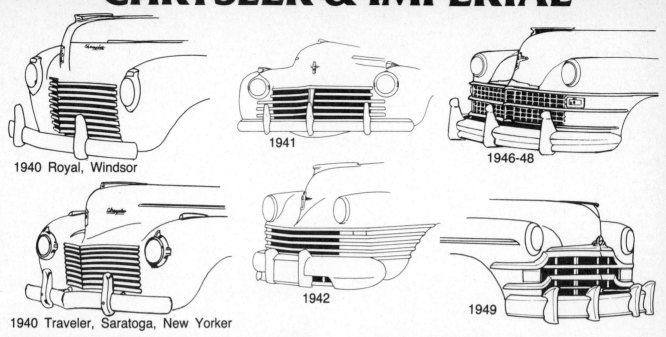

1940 Royal, Windsor

1941

1946-48

1940 Traveler, Saratoga, New Yorker

1942

1949

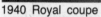

1940 Royal coupe

1940 Saratoga 4-door sedan

1941 Town & Country wagon

CHRYSLER & IMPERIAL

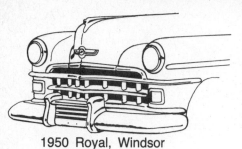

1950 Royal, Windsor

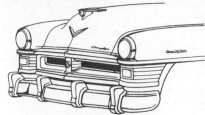

1951-52 Windsor

1951-52 New Yorker

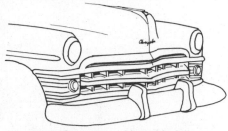

1950 Saratoga, New Yorker,
Town & Country, Crown Imperial

1951-52 Saratoga

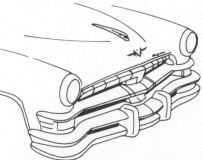

1951-52 Imperial, Crown Imperial

1941 Crown Imperial 8-passenger sedan

1946-48 Crown Imperial limousine

1942 New Yorker 4-door sedan

1946-48 Town & Country 4-door sedan

1946-48 Town & Country convertible

1946-48 New Yorker convertible

CHRYSLER & IMPERIAL

1953 New Yorker

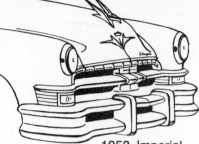
1953 Imperial

1954 New Yorker

1953 Windsor

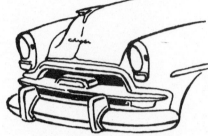
1954 Windsor

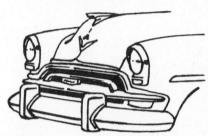
1954 New Yorker Deluxe

1946-48 Saratoga 4-door sedan

1946-48 Windsor 8-passenger sedan

1946-48 Saratoga club coupe

1949 Town & Country convertible

1946-48 Windsor convertible

1949 Saratoga club coupe

CHRYSLER & IMPERIAL

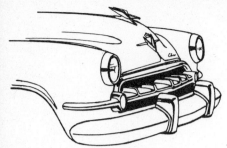

1954 Imperial

1955 New Yorker

1955-56 Imperial

1955 Windsor

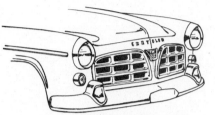

1955-56 300, 300B

1956 Windsor

1949 Royal 4-door sedan

1950 Royal Town & Country all-steel wagon

1950 Windsor Newport hardtop coupe

1951 New Yorker 4-door sedan

1950 Royal Town & Country wood-body wagon

1951 Windsor Town & Country wagon

CHRYSLER & IMPERIAL

1956 New Yorker

1957 300C, 1958 300D

1958 Windsor,
New Yorker, Saratoga

1957 Windsor,
New Yorker, Saratoga

1957 Imperial

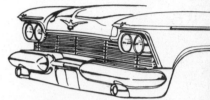
1958 Imperial

1951 Windsor Deluxe 4-door sedan

1953 New Yorker Deluxe convertible

1952 Windsor club coupe

1953 New Yorker Newport hardtop coupe

1953 Custom Imperial Newport hardtop coupe

1953 Windsor Deluxe 4-door sedan

CHRYSLER & IMPERIAL

1959 Windsor, Saratoga

1959 300E

1960 Windsor, Saratoga

1959 New Yorker

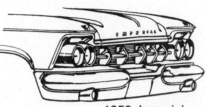
1959 Imperial

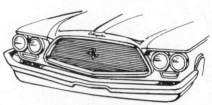
1960 New Yorker

1954 Custom Imperial 4-door sedan

1955 Windsor Deluxe Nassau hardtop coupe

1954 Custom Imperial Newport hardtop coupe

1955 Windsor Deluxe Town & Country wagon

1955 C300 hardtop coupe

1955 New Yorker Deluxe St. Regis hardtop coupe

CHRYSLER & IMPERIAL

1960 300F

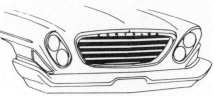
1961 Newport, Windsor

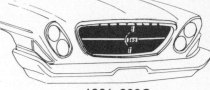
1961 300G

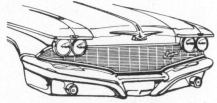
1960 Imperial

1961 New Yorker

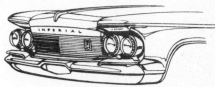
1961 Imperial

1955 Windsor Deluxe convertible

1956 Windsor convertible

1955 New Yorker Deluxe convertible

1957 New Yorker hardtop coupe

1956 Imperial 4-door sedan

1957 New Yorker Town & Country wagon

CHRYSLER & IMPERIAL

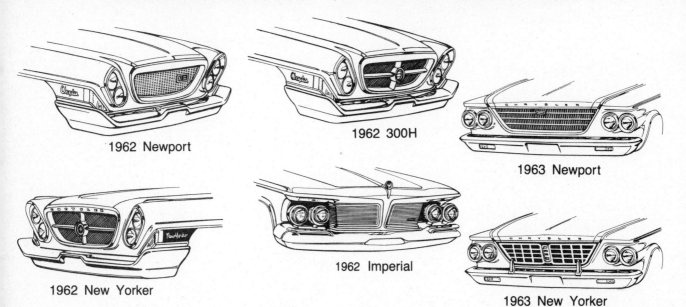

1962 Newport

1962 300H

1963 Newport

1962 New Yorker

1962 Imperial

1963 New Yorker

1957 Windsor hardtop sedan

1957 300C hardtop coupe

1958 Imperial Crown Southampton hardtop sedan

1958 Imperial LeBaron 4-door sedan

1958 300D hardtop coupe

1958 New Yorker convertible

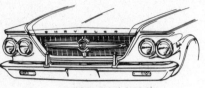
1963 300, 300J

1964 Newport

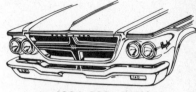
1964 300, 300K

1963 Imperial

1964 New Yorker

1964 Imperial

1958 Saratoga hardtop coupe

1959 Windsor hardtop coupe

1959 300E hardtop coupe

1960 Imperial Custom Southampton hardtop sedan

1959 Saratoga 4-door sedan

1960 Imperial Crown 4-door sedan

CHRYSLER & IMPERIAL

1965 Newport

1965 300, 300L

1966 Newport

1965 New Yorker

1965 Imperial

1966 New Yorker

1961 300G hardtop coupe

1961 300G convertible

1961 Imperial Crown Southampton hardtop sedan

1962 300H convertible

1962 Imperial LeBaron Southampton hardtop sedan

1963 300J hardtop coupe

The 1963 Chrysler 300J, available only as a hardtop coupe that year, can be identified by the letter "J" in the grille medallion.

CHRYSLER & IMPERIAL

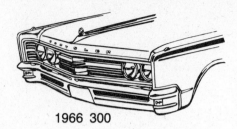
1966 300

1967 Newport

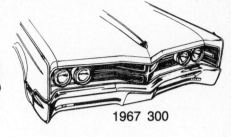
1967 300

1966 Imperial

1967 New Yorker

1967 Imperial

1963 Imperial LeBaron Southampton hardtop sedan

1966 Imperial Crown convertible

1963 300 convertible

1967 Newport Custom hardtop coupe

1964 Imperial Crown hardtop sedan

1968 300 hardtop coupe

CHRYSLER & IMPERIAL

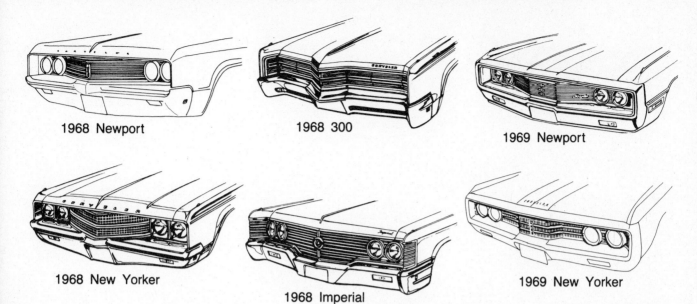

1968 Newport

1968 300

1969 Newport

1968 New Yorker

1968 Imperial

1969 New Yorker

1968 Imperial Crown hardtop coupe

1968 Imperial Crown convertible

1968 Newport Town & Country wagon

1968 Newport convertible

1969 Imperial LeBaron hardtop sedan

1969 Newport Custom hardtop sedan

CHRYSLER & IMPERIAL

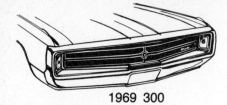
1969 300

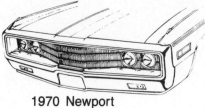
1970 Newport

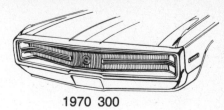
1970 300

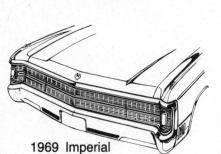
1969 Imperial

1970 New Yorker

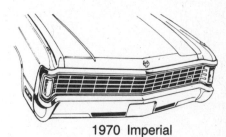
1970 Imperial

1970 Newport Custom hardtop sedan

1971 Newport hardtop coupe

1970 Imperial LeBaron hardtop sedan

1971 Imperial LeBaron hardtop sedan

1970 Town & Country wagon

1971 Imperial LeBaron hardtop sedan

CHRYSLER & IMPERIAL

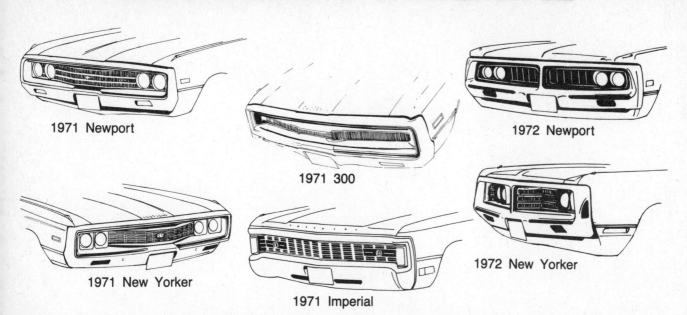

1971 Newport

1971 300

1972 Newport

1971 New Yorker

1971 Imperial

1972 New Yorker

1972 Newport Royal hardtop coupe

1972 Imperial LeBaron hardtop coupe

1972 Town & Country wagon

1973 New Yorker 4-door sedan

1972 New Yorker Brougham hardtop sedan

1973 Imperial LeBaron hardtop sedan

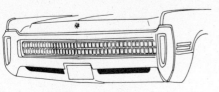

1972 Imperial

1973 New Yorker

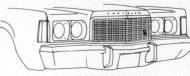

1974 Newport

1973 Newport

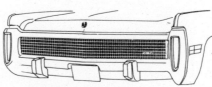

1973 Imperial

1974 New Yorker

1974 Newport hardtop coupe

1974 New Yorker hardtop sedan

1974 Imperial LeBaron hardtop sedan

1975 New Yorker Brougham hardtop coupe

1975 Cordoba coupe

1975 Cordoba coupe

CHRYSLER & IMPERIAL

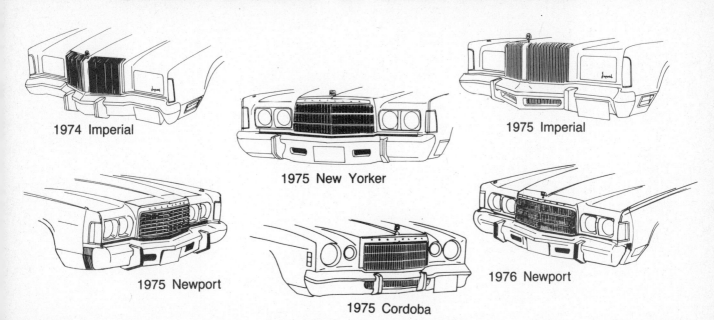

1974 Imperial

1975 New Yorker

1975 Imperial

1975 Newport

1975 Cordoba

1976 Newport

1975 Imperial LeBaron Crown coupe

1975 Imperial LeBaron hardtop coupe

1976 New Yorker Brougham hardtop sedan

1976 Cordoba coupe

1977 Newport hardtop sedan

1977 New Yorker Brougham hardtop sedan

CHRYSLER & IMPERIAL

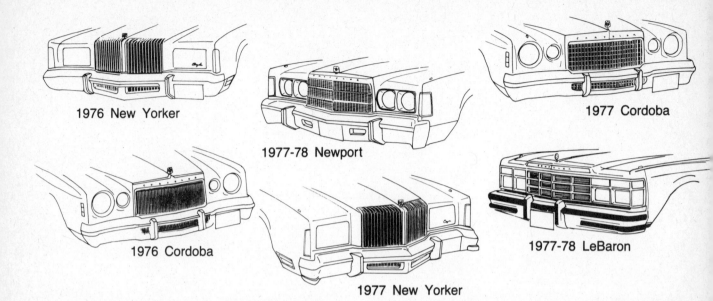

1976 New Yorker

1977-78 Newport

1977 Cordoba

1976 Cordoba

1977 New Yorker

1977-78 LeBaron

1977 Cordoba coupe

1978 Newport hardtop coupe

1977 Cordoba coupe

1978 New Yorker Brougham hardtop sedan

1977 LeBaron Medallion coupe

1978 New Yorker Brougham hardtop sedan

CHRYSLER & IMPERIAL

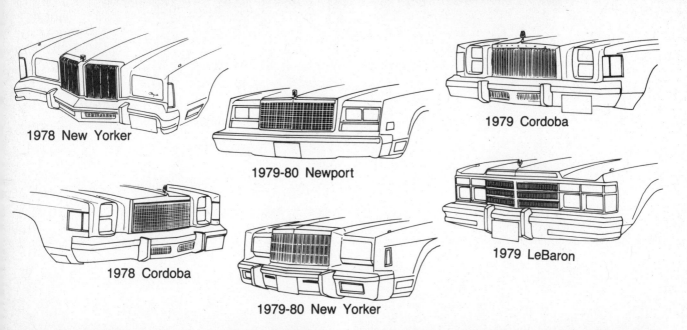

1978 New Yorker

1979-80 Newport

1979 Cordoba

1978 Cordoba

1979-80 New Yorker

1979 LeBaron

1978 Cordoba coupe

1979 New Yorker Fifth Avenue Edition sedan

1978 LeBaron Medallion coupe

1979 New Yorker Fifth Avenue Edition sedan

1978 LeBaron Medallion 4-door sedan

1979 LeBaron Town & Country wagon

CHRYSLER & IMPERIAL

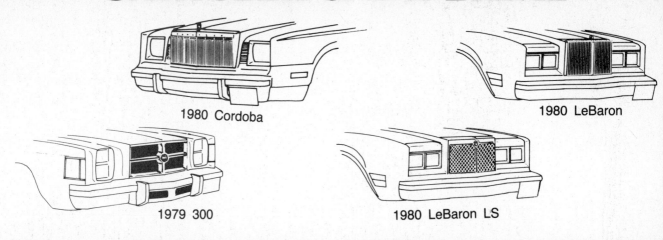

1980 Cordoba

1980 LeBaron

1979 300

1980 LeBaron LS

1979 Newport 4-door sedan

1979 LeBaron Medallion coupe

1980 Cordoba Crown coupe

1980 LeBaron Town & Country wagon

1979 Newport 4-door sedan

1979 Cordoba coupe

1980 LeBaron Medallion 4-door sedan

1980 New Yorker 4-door sedan

CROSLEY

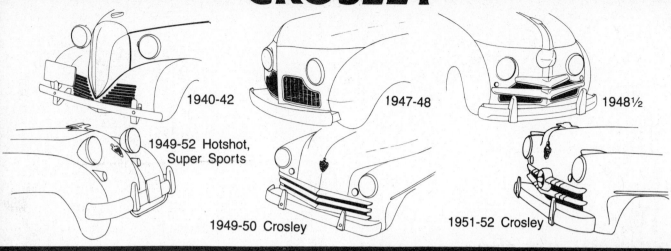

1940-42   1947-48   1948½

1949-52 Hotshot,
Super Sports

1949-50 Crosley   1951-52 Crosley

1940 Series 2A 2-door wagon

1947 Series CC Four 2-door wagon

1940 Series 2A convertible coupe

1949 Series CD Four Deluxe 2-door sedan

1946 Series CC Four 2-door sedan

1951 Series CD Four Super Sports roadster

DE SOTO

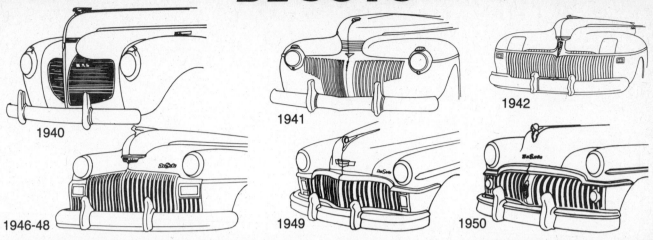

1940

1941

1942

1946-48

1949

1950

1940 Custom club coupe

1941 Custom 4-door sedan

1942 Custom convertible

1946-48 Custom Suburban 8-passenger sedan

1946-48 Custom 4-door sedan

1946-48 Custom club coupe

1949 Custom 4-door sedan

1950 Deluxe Carry-All 4-door sedan

DE SOTO

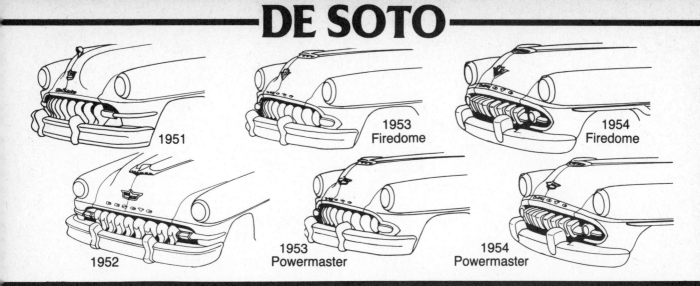

1951

1952

1953 Firedome

1953 Powermaster

1954 Firedome

1954 Powermaster

1951 Custom Suburban 8-passenger sedan

1952 Firedome 4-door sedan

1953 Firedome 8-passenger sedan

1954 Firedome convertible

1955 Fireflite Sportsman hardtop coupe

1956 Fireflite Adventurer hardtop coupe

1957 Fireflite convertible

1957 Fireflite Sportsman hardtop sedan

DE SOTO

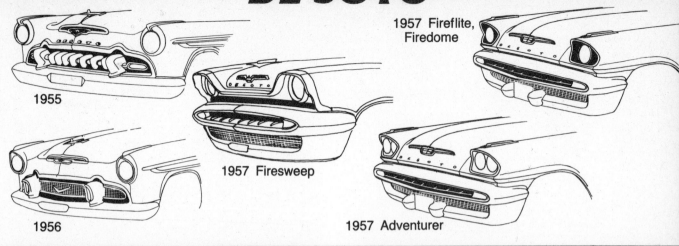

1955

1956

1957 Fireflite, Firedome

1957 Firesweep

1957 Adventurer

1957 Firedome convertible

1957 Fireflite Shopper wagon

1957 Firedome Sportsman hardtop coupe

1958 Firesweep Sportsman hardtop coupe

1958 Firedome 4-door sedan

1959 Firedome Sportsman hardtop sedan

1959 Fireflite Sportsman hardtop coupe

1959 Fireflite Sportsman hardtop coupe

DE SOTO

1958 Fireflite, Firedome, Adventurer

1958 Firesweep

1959

1960

1961

1959 Fireflite Sportsman hardtop sedan

1960 Adventurer 4-door sedan

1960 Adventurer hardtop coupe

1960 Adventurer hardtop coupe

1960 Adventurer hardtop sedan

1960 Fireflite 4-door sedan

1961 hardtop sedan

1961 hardtop coupe

DODGE

1940

1942

1949

1941

1946-48

1950

1940 DeLuxe 2-door sedan

1941 Custom convertible coupe

1941 Custom 4-door sedan

1942 DeLuxe club coupe

1946-48 Custom Town Sedan

1949 Coronet wood-body wagon

1949 Coronet 4-door sedan

1949 Wayfarer coupe

DODGE

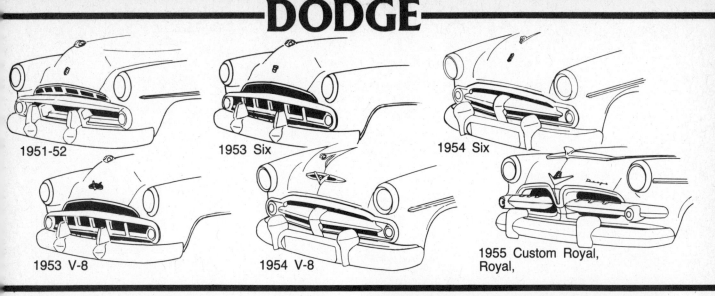

1951-52   1953 Six   1954 Six

1953 V-8   1954 V-8   1955 Custom Royal, Royal,

1949 Wayfarer roadster

1950 Coronet Diplomat hardtop coupe

1950 Coronet wood-body wagon

1950 Coronet 4-door sedan

1953 Coronet 4-door sedan

1954 Royal convertible

1954 Royal club coupe

1955 Custom Royal Lancer hardtop coupe

DODGE

1955 Coronet

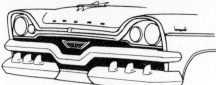
1957 Custom Royal

1958 Custom Royal, Royal, Coronet

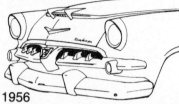
1956

1957 Royal, Coronet

1958½ Custom Royal

1955 Royal 4-door sedan

1956 Custom Royal Lancer "La Femme" hardtop coupe

1955 Custom Royal Lancer hardtop coupe

1956 Sierra Custom 4-door wagon

1956 Custom Royal convertible

1957 Custom Royal Lancer hardtop coupe

1956 Custom Royal Lancer hardtop sedan

1957 Custom Royal Lancer hardtop sedan

DODGE

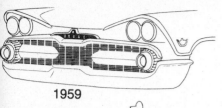
1959

1960 Dart

1961 Dart

1960 Polara, Matador

1961 Polara

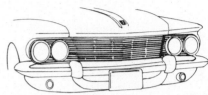
1961 Lancer

1957 Custom Royal convertible

1957 Custom Royal 4-door sedan

1957 Coronet 2-door sedan

1957 Sierra 4-door wagon

1958 Custom Royal Lancer hardtop coupe

1960 Matador hardtop sedan

1960 Matador 4-door sedan

1960 Dart Phoenix hardtop sedan

DODGE

1962 Polara, Dart

1962 Lancer

1963 Custom 880

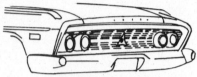
1962 Custom 880

1963 Polara, 330, 440

1960 Dart Seneca 2-door sedan

1961 Dart Pioneer wagon

1960 Dart Phoenix hardtop coupe

1961 Dart Phoenix convertible

1961 Lancer 770 hardtop coupe

1961 Polara hardtop sedan

1961 Lancer 770 hardtop coupe

1962 Polara 500 convertible

1963 Dart

DODGE

1964 Polara, 330, 440

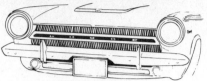

1964 Dart

1965 Coronet

1964 Custom 880

1965 Monaco, Polara

1965 Dart

1962 Dart 440 hardtop sedan

1962 Lancer GT hardtop coupe

1962 Custom 880 hardtop sedan

1962 Lancer 770 4-door sedan

1963 Dart 270 convertible

1963 Custom 880 hardtop sedan

1964 Custom 880 convertible

1964 Custom 880 hardtop coupe

1966 Monaco, Polara

1966 Coronet 500

1966-67 Charger

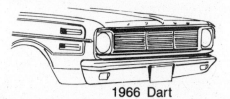

1966 Coronet, Coronet 440

1966 Dart

1967 Monaco

1964 Dart GT hardtop coupe

1964 Dart GT hardtop coupe

1965 Monaco hardtop coupe

1965 Monaco hardtop coupe

1966 Polara hardtop sedan

1966 Coronet 500 hardtop coupe

1966 Dart GT convertible

1967 Monaco hardtop sedan

DODGE

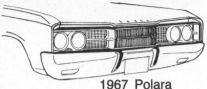
1967 Polara

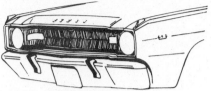
1967 Dart

1968 Polara

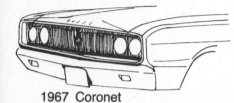
1967 Coronet

1968 Monaco

1968 Coronet

1967 Polara 500 hardtop coupe

1968 Polara hardtop sedan

1967 Polara convertible

1968 Polara hardtop sedan

1967 Coronet R/T hardtop coupe

1968 Coronet R/T hardtop coupe

1967 Dart GT convertible

1968 Coronet Super Bee coupe

DODGE

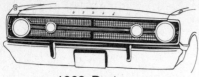

1968 Dart

1968 Charger

1969 Monaco

1969 Polara

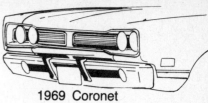

1969 Coronet

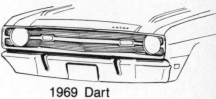

1969 Dart

1968 Coronet 440 hardtop coupe

1968 Coronet 440 hardtop coupe

1968 Dart GTS hardtop coupe

1968 Dart GTS hardtop coupe

1968 Coronet Super Bee coupe

1969 Polara 500 hardtop coupe

1969 Polara wagon

1969 Coronet R/T hardtop coupe

DODGE

1969 Charger

1970 Polara

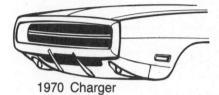

1970 Dart

1970 Monaco

1970 Coronet

1970 Charger

1969 Dart Swinger 340 hardtop coupe

1969 Charger Daytona hardtop coupe

1969 Dart GT hardtop coupe

1970 Monaco wagon

1969 Charger hardtop coupe

1970 Coronet 500 hardtop coupe

1969 Charger 500 hardtop coupe

1970 Coronet 500 hardtop coupe

DODGE

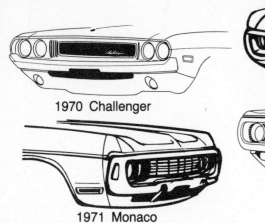

1970 Challenger

1971 Polara

1971 Dart, Demon

1971 Coronet

1971 Monaco

1971 Charger

1970 Challenger R/T convertible

1971 Dart Swinger hardtop coupe

1970 Charger R/T hardtop coupe

1971 Dart Custom 4-door sedan

1971 Polara Brougham hardtop sedan

1971 Demon 340 coupe

1971 Coronet Brougham 4-door sedan

1971 Demon coupe

112

DODGE

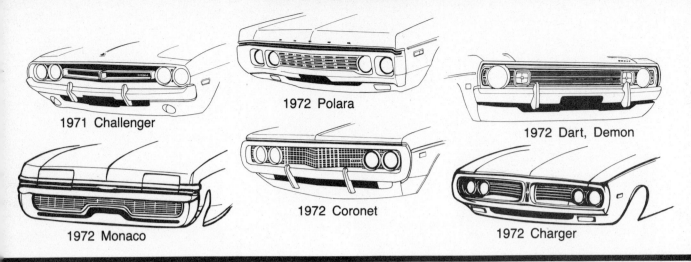

1971 Challenger

1972 Polara

1972 Dart, Demon

1972 Monaco

1972 Coronet

1972 Charger

1971 Charger 500 hardtop coupe

1971 Charger R/T hardtop coupe

1971 Charger SE hardtop coupe

1971 Challenger R/T hardtop coupe

1972 Polara Custom hardtop sedan

1972 Coronet Custom 4-door sedan

1972 Dart Demon coupe

DODGE

1972 Challenger

1973 Polara

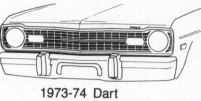
1973-74 Dart

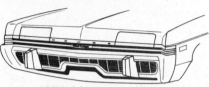
1973 Monaco

1973 Coronet

1973-74 Charger

1972 Charger SE hardtop coupe

1972 Challenger hardtop coupe

1973 Monaco hardtop coupe

1973 Polara Custom hardtop sedan

1973 Coronet Custom 4-door sedan

1973 Dart Swinger hardtop coupe

1973 Dart Swinger hardtop coupe

DODGE

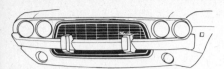
1973-74 Challenger

1974 Coronet

1975-76 Coronet

1974 Monaco

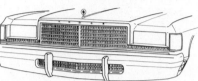
1975-76 Royal Monaco

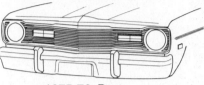
1975-76 Dart

1973 Challenger hardtop coupe

1974 Charger SE coupe

1974 Dart Sport coupe

1974 Challenger Rallye hardtop coupe

1974 Dart Custom 4-door sedan

1975 Royal Monaco Brougham coupe

1974 Charger SE coupe

1975 Coronet Brougham hardtop coupe

DODGE

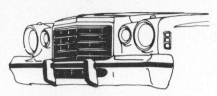

1975-76 Charger SE, Daytona

1976-77 Aspen

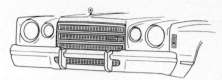

1977-78 Charger

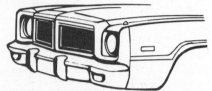

1975-76 Charger, Charger Sport

1977-78 Monaco

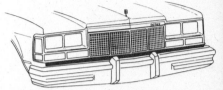

1977-78 Diplomat

1975 Dart Sport coupe

1976 Dart Lite coupe

1975 Charger Special Edition coupe

1976 Charger Daytona coupe

1976 Royal Monaco 4-door sedan

1976 Aspen wagon

1976 Coronet Custom 4-door sedan

1976 Aspen Special Edition coupe

DODGE

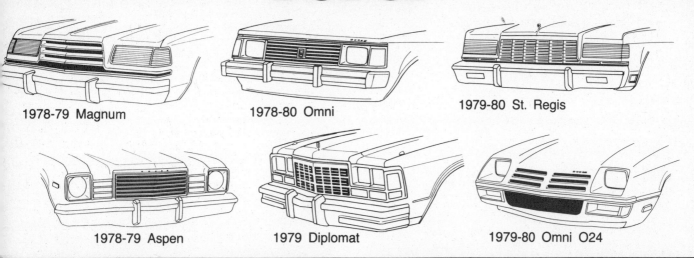

1978-79 Magnum   1978-80 Omni   1979-80 St. Regis

1978-79 Aspen   1979 Diplomat   1979-80 Omni O24

1977 Royal Monaco Brougham 4-door sedan

1977 Aspen R/T Super Pak coupe

1977 Aspen Custom coupe

1977 Aspen Special Edition wagon

1977 Charger Special Edition coupe

1978 Magnum XE coupe

1978 Monaco Brougham 4-door sedan

1978 Aspen R/T coupe

DODGE

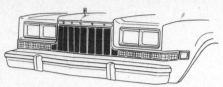

1980 Diplomat

1980 Mirada

1980 Aspen

1978 Charger Special Edition coupe

1978 Omni sedan

1979 St. Regis 4-door sedan

1979 Aspen R/T coupe

1979 Omni sedan

1979 Omni 024 hatchback coupe

1979 St. Regis 4-door sedan

1980 Mirada coupe

EDSEL

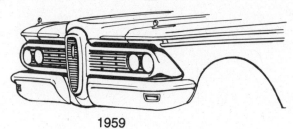
1959

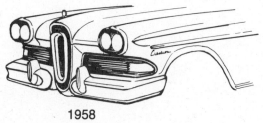
1958

1960

1958 Citation hardtop sedan

1959 Ranger 4-door sedan

1958 Corsair hardtop sedan

1960 Ranger convertible

1959 Corsair hardtop sedan

1960 Villager wagon

1965-69 Series I

1975-79 Series III

1970-74 Series II

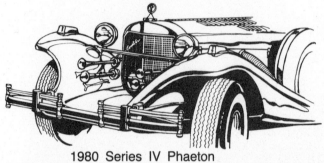
1980 Series IV Phaeton

Series I phaeton

Series I SSK roadster

Series II phaeton

Series III phaeton

Series III roadster

Series IV phaeton

FORD

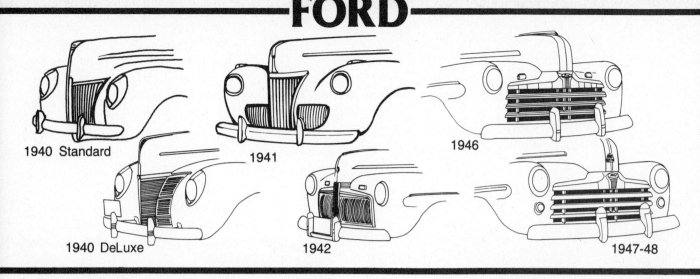

1940 Standard 1941 1946
1940 DeLuxe 1942 1947-48

1940 V8/85 DeLuxe Fordor sedan

1942 V8 Super DeLuxe sedan coupe

1942 V8 Super DeLuxe wagon

1946 V8 Super DeLuxe Sportsman convertible

1948 DeLuxe Fordor sedan

1948 Super DeLuxe wagon

1948 Super DeLuxe convertible

121

FORD

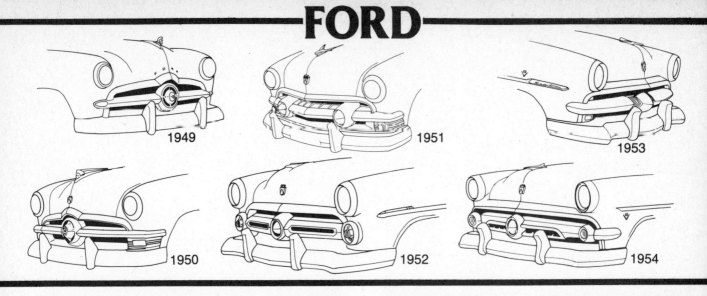

1949 1951 1953
1950 1952 1954

1949 Custom Tudor sedan

1949 Custom wagon

1950 Custom Crestliner Tudor sedan

1950 Custom convertible

1951 Custom Victoria hardtop coupe

1951 Custom Victoria hardtop coupe

1951 DeLuxe business coupe

FORD

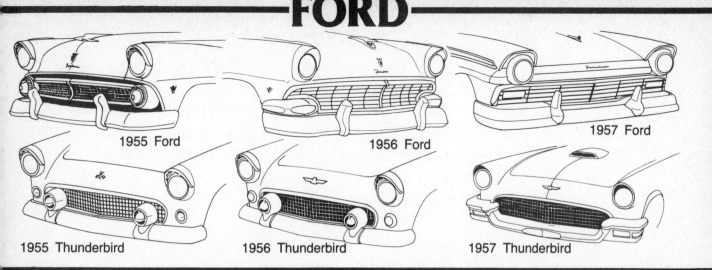

1955 Ford   1956 Ford   1957 Ford

1955 Thunderbird   1956 Thunderbird   1957 Thunderbird

1952 Crestline Sunliner convertible

1953 Crestline Victoria hardtop coupe

1953 Crestline Sunliner convertible

1954 Crestline Country Squire 4-door wagon

1954 Crestline Skyliner hardtop coupe

1955 Fairlane Crown Victoria coupe

1955 Thunderbird convertible (prototype)

1955 Fairlane Town Sedan

FORD

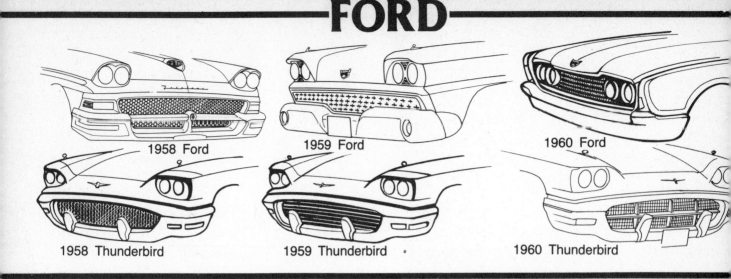

1958 Ford   1959 Ford   1960 Ford

1958 Thunderbird   1959 Thunderbird   1960 Thunderbird

1956 Thunderbird convertible

1956 Fairlane Sunliner convertible (prototype)

1956 Fairlane Town Victoria hardtop sedan

1957 Fairlane 500 Skyliner hardtop/convertible

1957 Country Squire 4-door wagon

1957 Fairlane 500 Skyliner hardtop/convertible

1957 Fairlane 500 Town Victoria hardtop sedan

1957 Del Rio Ranch Wagon

FORD

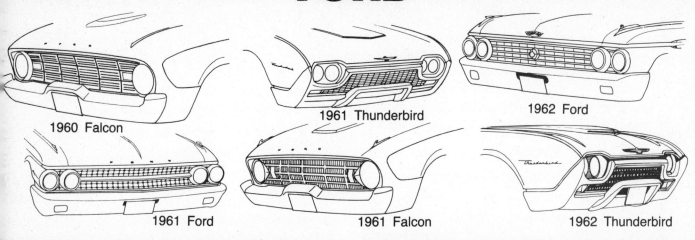

1960 Falcon   1961 Thunderbird   1962 Ford

1961 Ford   1961 Falcon   1962 Thunderbird

1957 Thunderbird convertible with hardtop

1957 Thunderbird convertible

1958 Thunderbird hardtop coupe

1959 Country Squire 4-door wagon

1959 Thunderbird hardtop coupe

1959 Thunderbird convertible

1960 Fairlane 500 Town Sedan

1960 2-door Ranch Wagon

FORD

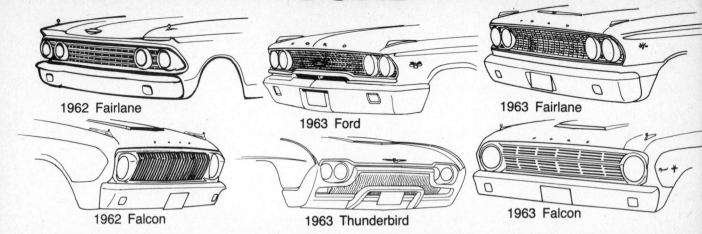

1962 Fairlane   1963 Ford   1963 Fairlane

1962 Falcon   1963 Thunderbird   1963 Falcon

1960 Falcon 2-door sedan

1960 Falcon 2-door wagon

1960 Thunderbird hardtop coupe

1961 Galaxie Town Sedan

1961 Galaxie Sunliner convertible

1961 Falcon 4-door sedan

1961 Falcon 4-door wagon

1961 Thunderbird hardtop coupe

FORD

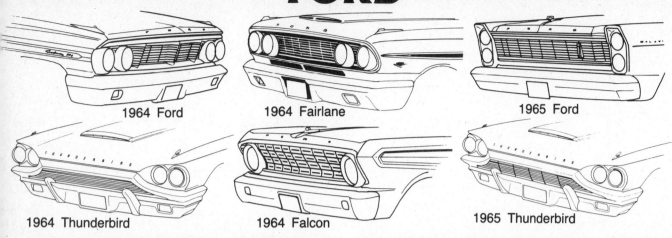

1964 Ford   1964 Fairlane   1965 Ford

1964 Thunderbird   1964 Falcon   1965 Thunderbird

1961 Thunderbird convertible

1962 Galaxie 500XL Sunliner convertible

1962 Galaxie Club Sedan

1962 Falcon Futura coupe

1962 Falcon Futura coupe

1963 Galaxie 500 hardtop coupe

1963 Falcon Futura Sprint hardtop coupe

1963 Thunderbird hardtop coupe

FORD

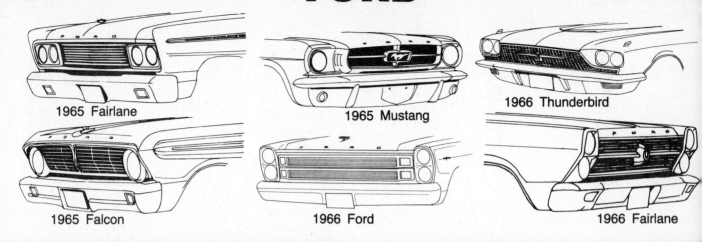

1965 Fairlane   1965 Mustang   1966 Thunderbird

1965 Falcon   1966 Ford   1966 Fairlane

1964 Galaxie 500 hardtop sedan

1964 Galaxie 500XL hardtop coupe

1964 Falcon Futura Sprint convertible

1964 Falcon Futura Sprint hardtop coupe

1964 Thunderbird Landau hardtop coupe

1965 Galaxie 500XL hardtop coupe

1965 Galaxie 500 LTD hardtop sedan

1965 Falcon Futura convertible

FORD

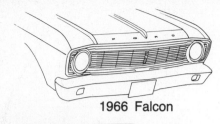

1966 Falcon

1967 Ford

1967 Fairlane

1966 Mustang

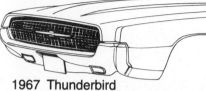

1967 Thunderbird

1967 Falcon

1965 Mustang GT 2+2 fastback coupe

1965 Mustang convertible

1965 Mustang hardtop coupe

1966 Country Squire 4-door wagon

1966 Falcon Futura Sports Coupe

1966 Mustang hardtop coupe

1966 Mustang convertible

1966 LTD hardtop sedan

FORD

1967 Mustang
1968 Galaxie, Custom
1968 Fairlane, Torino
1968 LTD
1968 Thunderbird
1968-70 Falcon

1966 Mustang GT 2+2 fastback coupe

1967 Thunderbird hardtop coupe

1967 Galaxie 500XL fastback hardtop coupe

1968 Torino hardtop coupe

1967 Fairlane 500XL hardtop coupe

1968 Torino GT fastback hardtop coupe

1967 Mustang hardtop coupe

1968 Falcon Futura wagon

FORD

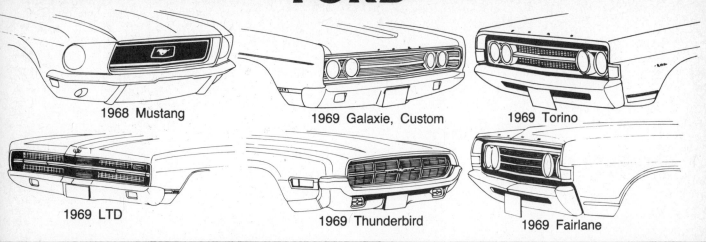

1968 Mustang

1969 Galaxie, Custom

1969 Torino

1969 LTD

1969 Thunderbird

1969 Fairlane

1968 Mustang convertible

1968 Thunderbird Landau sedan

1969 Galaxie 500 SportsRoof hardtop coupe

1969 LTD hardtop coupe

1969 Torino Cobra fastback hardtop coupe

1969 Torino 4-door sedan

1969 Fairlane 500 convertible

1969 Falcon Futura Sports Coupe

FORD

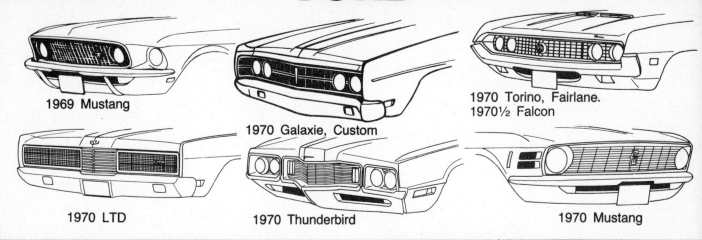

1969 Mustang

1970 Galaxie, Custom

1970 Torino, Fairlane.
1970½ Falcon

1970 LTD

1970 Thunderbird

1970 Mustang

1969 Mustang Mach I SportsRoof hardtop coupe

1970 Torino GT SportsRoof hardtop coupe

1969 Thunderbird Landau sedan

1970 Falcon Futura 4-door sedan

1970 LTD Brougham hardtop sedan

1970 Mustang Grande hardtop coupe

1970 Thunderbird Landau sedan

1970 Maverick 2-door sedan

FORD

1970 Mustang Mach I

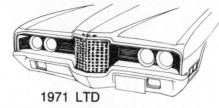

1971 LTD

1971 Thunderbird

1970-72 Maverick

1971 Galaxie, Custom

1971 Torino

1971 LTD Country Squire wagon

1971 Torino Squire wagon

1971 Mustang Mach I SportsRoof hardtop coupe

1971 Maverick 2-door sedan

1971 Pinto 2-door sedan

1972 LTD hardtop coupe

1972 Gran Torino hardtop coupe

1972 Thunderbird hardtop coupe

FORD

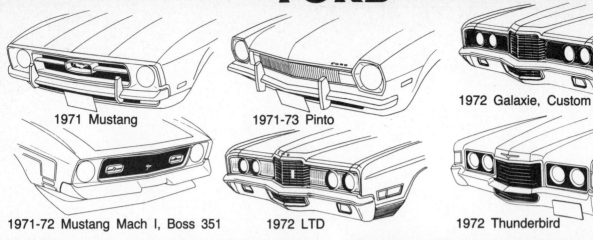

1971 Mustang

1971-73 Pinto

1972 Galaxie, Custom

1971-72 Mustang Mach I, Boss 351

1972 LTD

1972 Thunderbird

1972 Mustang Sprint SportsRoof hardtop coupe

1972 Maverick 2-door sedan

1972 Maverick 4-door sedan

1972 Pinto 2-door sedan

1973 LTD hardtop sedan

1973 Gran Torino Brougham 4-door pillared hardtop

1973 Mustang hardtop coupe

1973 Pinto Squire wagon

FORD

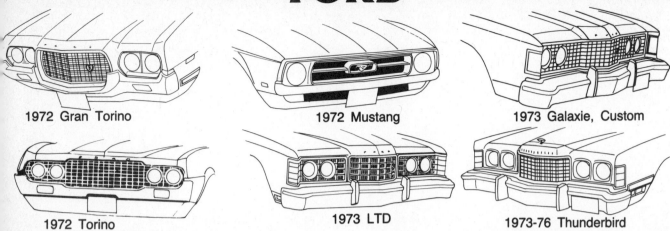

1972 Gran Torino   1972 Mustang   1973 Galaxie, Custom

1972 Torino   1973 LTD   1973-76 Thunderbird

1973 Thunderbird hardtop coupe

1974 LTD Brougham 4-door pillared hardtop

1974 Gran Torino wagon

1974 Mustang II Ghia coupe

1974 Mustang II hatchback coupe

1974 Maverick 4-door sedan

1974 Pinto Runabout sedan

1974 Thunderbird hardtop coupe

FORD

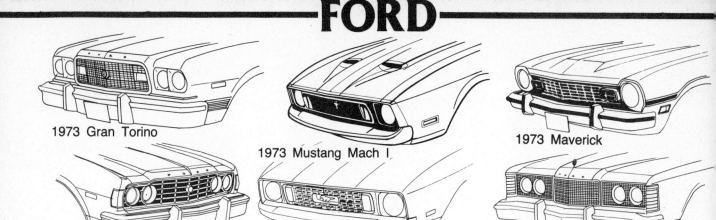

1973 Gran Torino

1973 Mustang Mach I

1973 Maverick

1973 Torino

1973 Mustang

1974 LTD

1975 LTD Landau 2-door pillared hardtop

1975 LTD 4-door pillared hardtop

1975 Granada 2-door sedan

1975 Elite hardtop coupe

1975 Mustang II Ghia coupe

1975 Thunderbird hardtop coupe

1976 LTD Landau 2-door pillared hardtop

1976 Gran Torino Brougham 4-door pillared hardtop

FORD

1974 Galaxie, Custom

1974-76 Gran Torino Elite

1974 Maverick

1974-76 Gran Torino, Torino

1974 Mustang II

1974-75 Pinto

1976 Ford Granada Ghia 4-door sedan

1976 Mustang II Cobra II fastback coupe

1976 Mustang II Ghia coupe

1976 Maverick Stallion 2-door sedan

1976 Pinto Stallion 2-door sedan

1976 Thunderbird hardtop coupe

1977 LTD II hardtop coupe

1977 LTD wagon

FORD

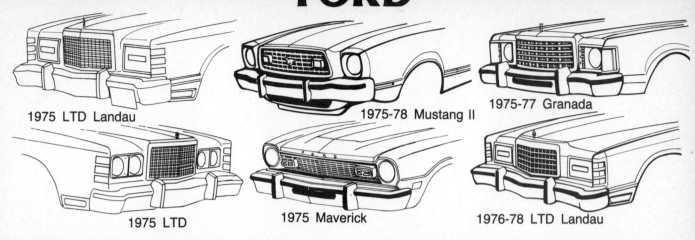

1975 LTD Landau   1975-78 Mustang II   1975-77 Granada

1975 LTD   1975 Maverick   1976-78 LTD Landau

1977 Granada Sports Coupe

1978 Fairmont 4-door sedan

1977 Mustang II hatchback coupe

1978 Fairmont 2-door sedan

1977 Pinto Runabout sedan

1978 Fairmont Squire wagon

1977 Thunderbird coupe

1978 Granada ESS 4-door sedan

FORD

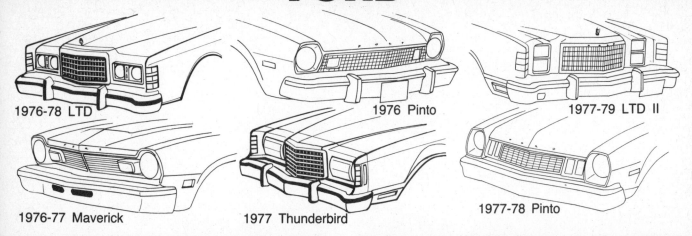

1976-78 LTD   1976 Pinto   1977-79 LTD II

1976-77 Maverick   1977 Thunderbird   1977-78 Pinto

1978 LTD II Brougham hardtop coupe

1978 Mustang II coupe

1978 Mustang II King Cobra hatchback coupe

1978 Thunderbird coupe

1979 Fairmont Futura coupe

1979 LTD Landau 2-door sedan

1979 LTD II Sports Touring hardtop coupe

1979 Fairmont Squire wagon

FORD

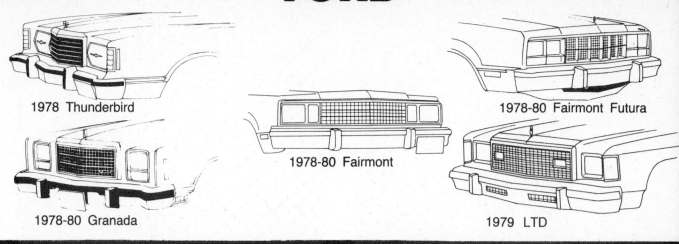

1978 Thunderbird

1978-80 Fairmont

1978-80 Fairmont Futura

1978-80 Granada

1979 LTD

1979 LTD 2-door sedan

1979 Thunderbird Heritage coupe

1979 LTD Country Squire wagon

1980 LTD 4-door sedan

1979 Mustang hatchback coupe

1980 Granada Ghia 4-door sedan

1979 Mustang Turbo hatchback coupe

1980 Fairmont Squire wagon

FORD

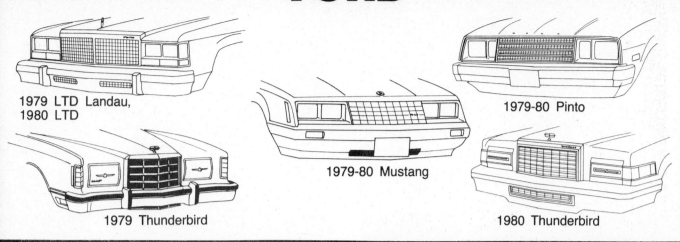

1979 LTD Landau,
1980 LTD

1979-80 Mustang

1979-80 Pinto

1979 Thunderbird

1980 Thunderbird

1980 Fairmont Turbo coupe (prototype)

1980 Mustang Cobra Turbo hatchback coupe

1980 Pinto wagon with Cruising Package

1980 Mustang Cobra Turbo hatchback coupe

1980 Pinto Squire wagon

1980 LTD Country Squire wagon

1980 Pinto Rallye hatchback sedan

1980 Thunderbird coupe

FRAZER

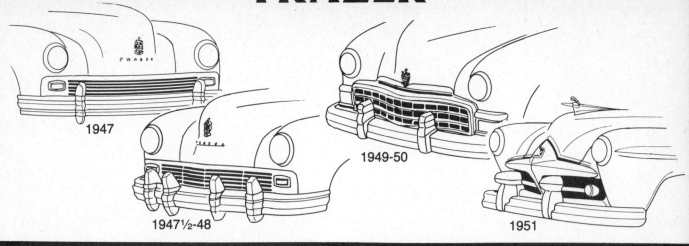

1947

1947½-48

1949-50

1951

1947 standard 4-door sedan

1948 Manhattan 4-door sedan

1948 standard 4-door sedan

1949-50 Manhattan 4-door sedan

1949-50 Manhattan 4-door sedan

1951 standard 4-door sedan

1951 Vagabond utility sedan

FRAZER

1948 Manhattan 4-door sedan

GRAHAM

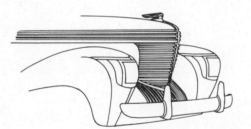

1940 Supercharger, Standard

1940-41 Hollywood Custom

1940 Supercharger Custom 4-door sedan

1940 Hollywood Custom Super 4-door sedan (prototype)

HENRY J

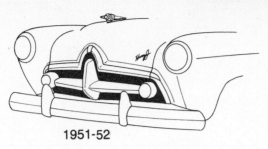

1951-52

1952-54

1951 standard (Four) 2-door sedan

1952 Vagabond DeLuxe (Six) 2-door sedan

1951 DeLuxe (Six) 2-door sedan

1953 Corsair (Four) 2-door sedan

1954 Corsair DeLuxe (Six) 2-door sedan

HUDSON

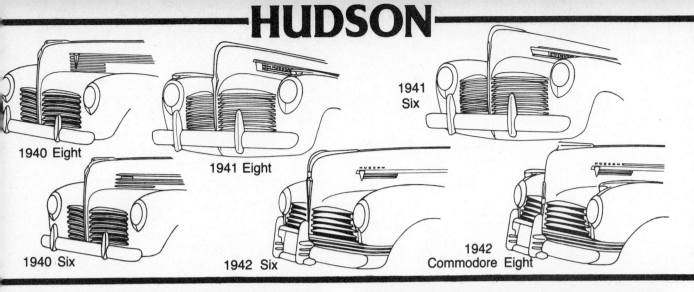

1940 Eight

1941 Eight

1941 Six

1940 Six

1942 Six

1942 Commodore Eight

1940 Eight convertible coupe

1942 Commodore Eight 4-door sedan

1946 Commodore Six 4-door sedan

1946 Super Six 4-door sedan

1948 Commodore Eight 4-door sedan

1948 Super Six club coupe

1948-49 Commodore Eight convertible brougham

HUDSON

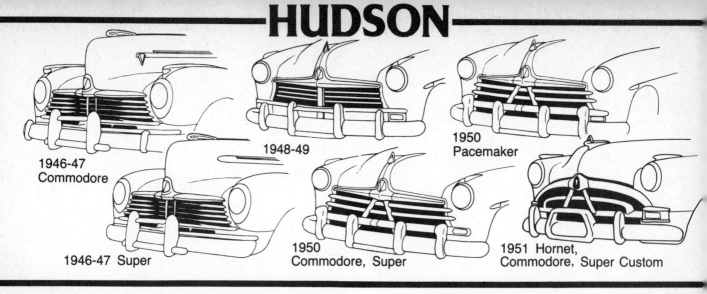

1946-47 Commodore

1948-49

1950 Pacemaker

1946-47 Super

1950 Commodore, Super

1951 Hornet, Commodore, Super Custom

1950 Pacemaker 4-door sedan

1951 Hornet 4-door sedan

1951 Pacemaker 4-door sedan

1951 Commodore Six Custom Hollywood hardtop coupe

1953 Super Wasp 4-door sedan

1953 Super Jet 4-door sedan

HUDSON

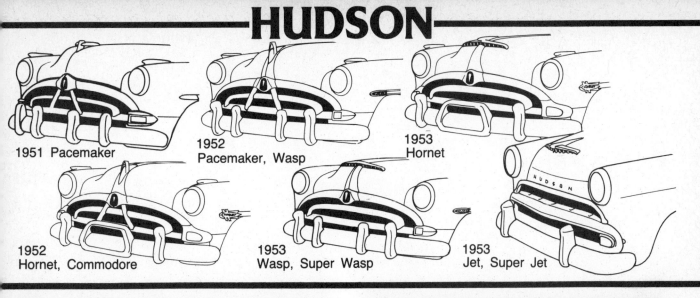

1951 Pacemaker

1952 Pacemaker, Wasp

1953 Hornet

1952 Hornet, Commodore

1953 Wasp, Super Wasp

1953 Jet, Super Jet

1953 Hornet 4-door sedan

1954 Super Wasp Hollywood hardtop coupe

1954-55 Italia coupe

1954 Super Wasp Hollywood hardtop coupe

1954 Jet Family Club Sedan

1954 Hornet Special 4-door sedan

1954 Super Jet 4-door sedan

HUDSON

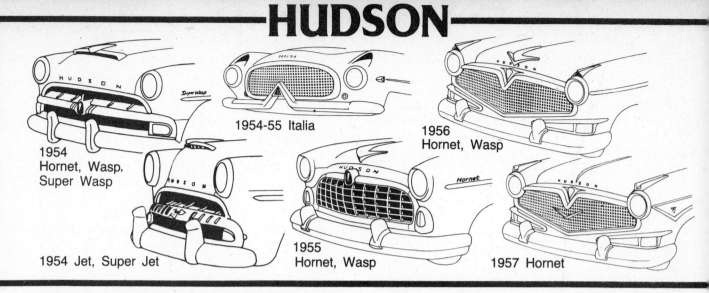

1954
Hornet, Wasp,
Super Wasp

1954-55 Italia

1956
Hornet, Wasp

1954 Jet, Super Jet

1955
Hornet, Wasp

1957 Hornet

1955 Wasp Custom 4-door sedan

1956 Hornet Custom 4-door sedan

1957 Hornet Custom 4-door sedan

HUPMOBILE

Prototype 1940 Skylark Custom 4-door sedan

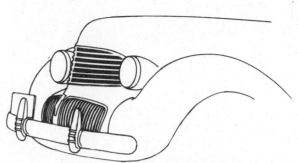

1940-41 Skylark Custom

Prototype 1940 Skylark Custom 4-door sedan

KAISER

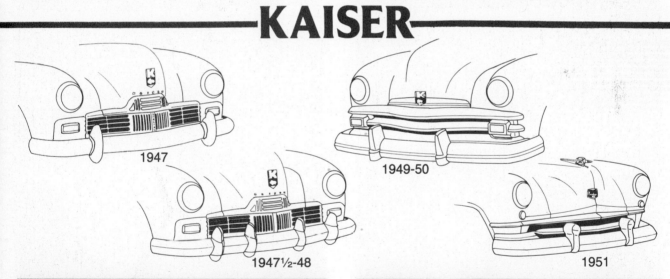

1947

1949-50

1947½-48

1951

1947 Custom 4-door sedan

1949 Deluxe 4-door sedan

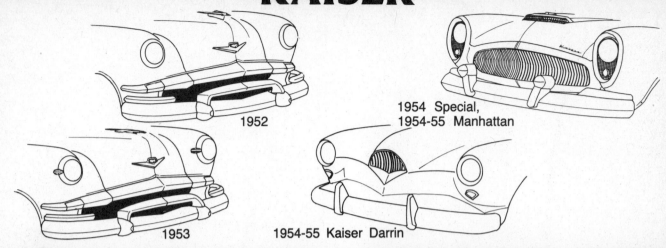

1952

1954 Special,
1954-55 Manhattan

1953

1954-55 Kaiser Darrin

1949-50 Virginian hardtop sedan

1949-50 Deluxe convertible sedan

1951 Deluxe 2-door sedan

1952 Virginian Deluxe club coupe

1953 "Hardtop" Dragon 4-door sedan

1954 Darrin DKF-161 roadster

1955 Manhattan 4-door sedan (prototype)

LA SALLE

1940 Series 52 Special coupe

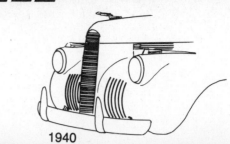

1940

1940 Series 52 Special convertible sedan

1940 Series 50 4-door sedan

LINCOLN

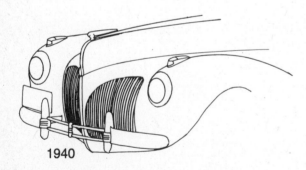

1940

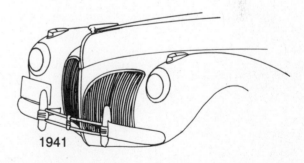

1941

1940 Zephyr 3-passenger coupe

1940 Continental club coupe

LINCOLN

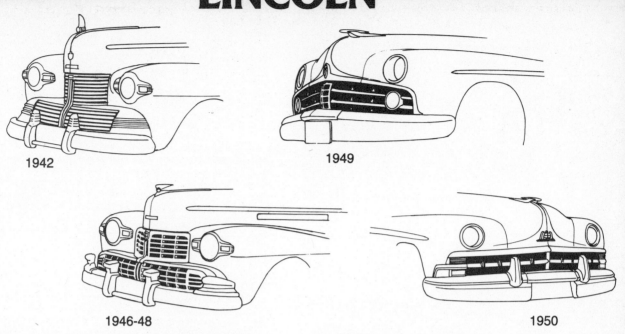

1942

1949

1946-48

1950

1940 Continental club coupe

1941 Continental club coupe

1941 Continental convertible coupe (cabriolet)

LINCOLN

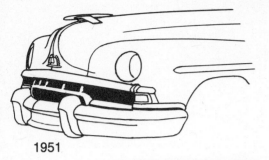
1951

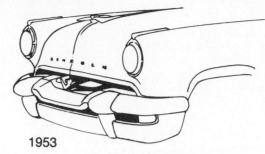
1953

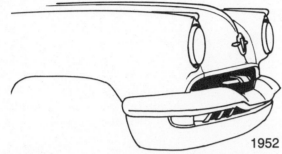
1952

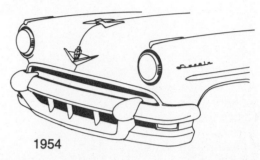
1954

1942 Continental convertible coupe (cabriolet)

1946 4-door sedan (Series 66H)

1946 Continental club coupe

1947 Continental club coupe

1946 convertible (Series 66H)

1948 4-door sedan (Series 876H)

153

LINCOLN

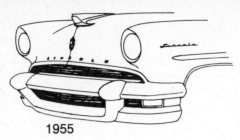
1955

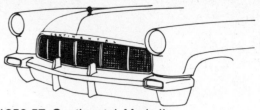
1956-57 Continental Mark II

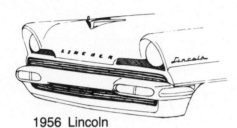
1956 Lincoln

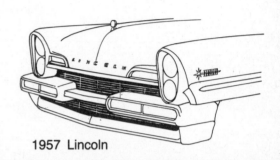
1957 Lincoln

1949 Cosmopolitan convertible

1953 Cosmopolitan Sport hardtop coupe

1951 coupe (Series 1EL)

1955 Custom Sport hardtop coupe

1951 Cosmopolitan Capri coupe

1956 Premiere hardtop coupe

LINCOLN

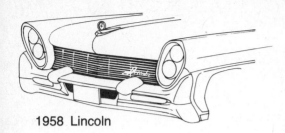

1958 Lincoln

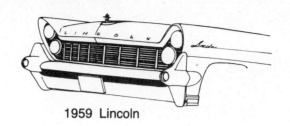

1959 Lincoln

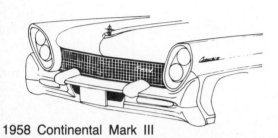

1958 Continental Mark III

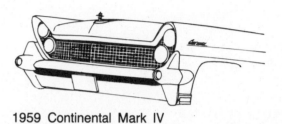

1959 Continental Mark IV

1956 Continental Mark II hardtop coupe

1957 Capri 4-door sedan

1957 Premiere convertible

1958 Continental Mark III Landau hardtop sedan

1957 Continental Mark II hardtop coupe

1958 Premiere Landau hardtop sedan

155

LINCOLN

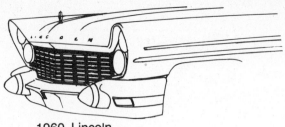
1960 Lincoln

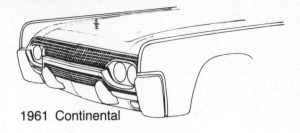
1961 Continental

1960 Continental Mark V

1962 Continental

1958 Continental Mark III Landau hardtop sedan

1960 Continental Mark V hardtop sedan

1959 Continental Mark IV hardtop coupe

1961 Continental hardtop sedan

1960 Premiere Landau hardtop sedan

1962 Continental convertible sedan

LINCOLN

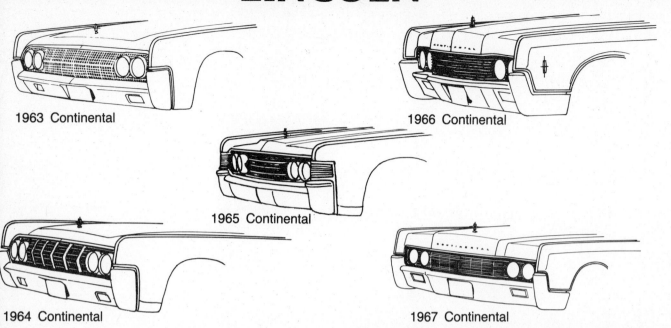

1963 Continental

1966 Continental

1965 Continental

1964 Continental

1967 Continental

1963 Continental convertible sedan

1966 Continental sedan

1963 Continental hardtop sedan

1967 Continental sedan

1964 Continental sedan

1968 Continental Mark III hardtop coupe

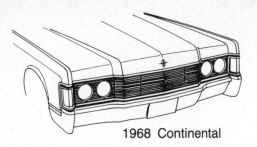

1968 Continental

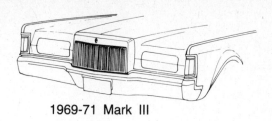

1969-71 Mark III

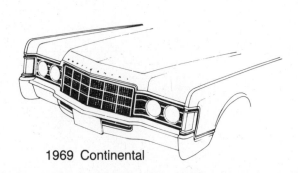

1969 Continental

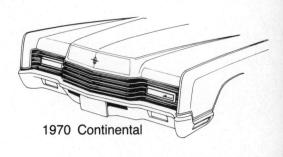

1970 Continental

1969 Continental hardtop coupe

1971 Continental sedan

1970 Continental Mark III hardtop coupe

1972 Continental Mark IV hardtop coupe

1971 Continental Mark III hardtop coupe

1973 Continental sedan

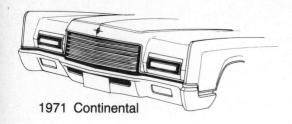
1971 Continental

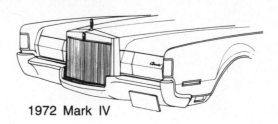
1972 Mark IV

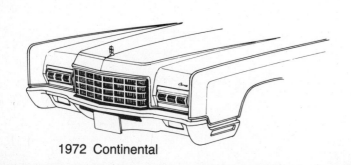
1972 Continental

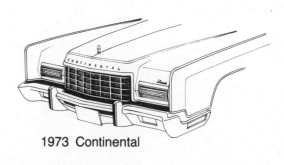
1973 Continental

1974 Continental Mark IV hardtop coupe

1976 Continental Town Coupe

1974 Continental Town Car sedan

1976 Continental Mark IV hardtop coupe

1975 Continental Mark IV hardtop coupe

1977 Continental Town Car sedan

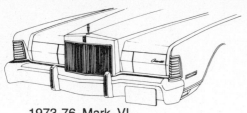

1973-76 Mark VI

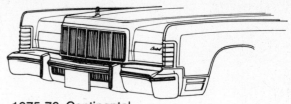

1975-76 Continental

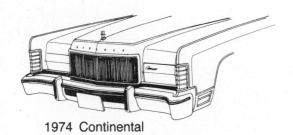

1974 Continental

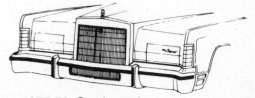

1977-79 Continental

1977 Continental Town Coupe

1978 Continental Williamsburg Town Car sedan

1977 Continental Mark V hardtop coupe

LINCOLN

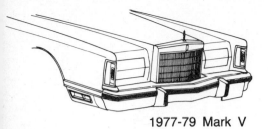
1977-79 Mark V

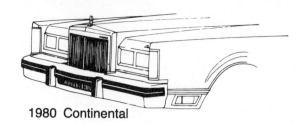
1980 Continental

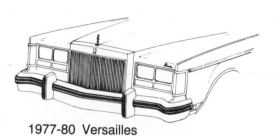
1977-80 Versailles

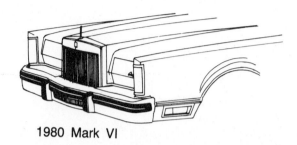
1980 Mark VI

1978 Versailles sedan

1979 Continental Town Car sedan

1979 Versailles sedan

1980 Continental Town Car sedan

1979 Continental Mark V Collector's Edition hardtop coupe

1980 Continental Mark VI hardtop coupe

MERCURY

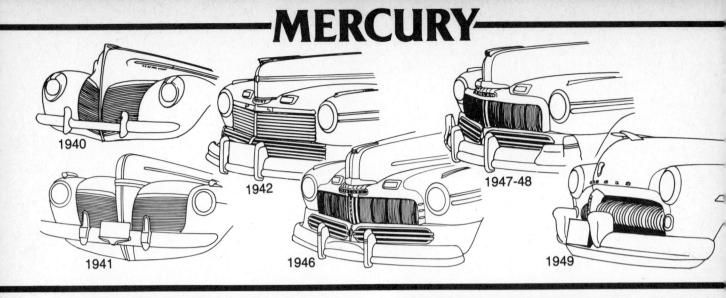

1940
1941
1942
1946
1947-48
1949

1940 convertible coupe

1940 convertible sedan

1941 Town Sedan

1942 Tudor Sedan

1946 Sportsman convertible

1947 Town Sedan

1949 wagon

MERCURY

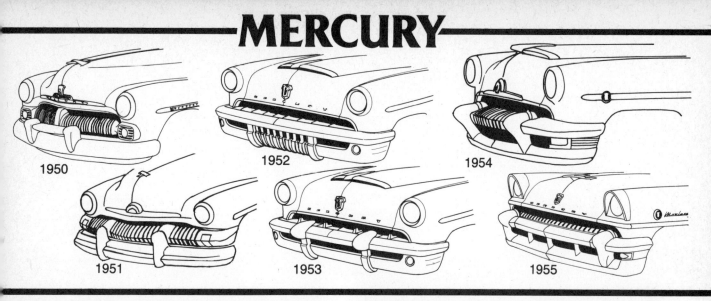

1950
1952
1954
1951
1953
1955

1949 convertible

1950 Monterey coupe

1950 wagon

1951 Sport Sedan

1952 Monterey hardtop coupe

1953 Monterey convertible

1954 Monterey hardtop coupe

1955 Monterey hardtop coupe

MERCURY

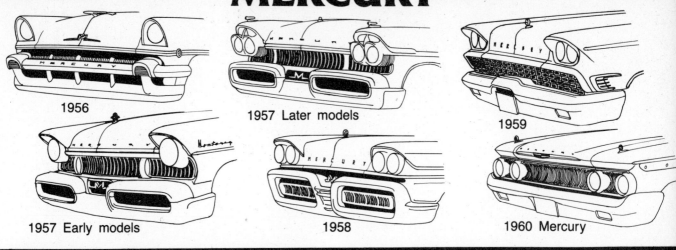

1956

1957 Later models

1959

1957 Early models

1958

1960 Mercury

1956 Monterey Sport Sedan

1957 Montclair Phaeton hardtop sedan

1957 Turnpike Cruiser convertible

1958 Park Lane Phaeton hardtop sedan

1959 Monterey 2-door sedan

1959 Colony Park hardtop wagon

1960 Montclair Cruiser hardtop sedan

1960 Monterey 2-door sedan

MERCURY

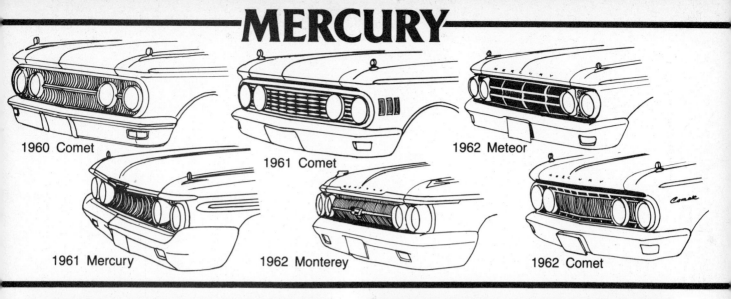

1960 Comet

1961 Comet

1962 Meteor

1961 Mercury

1962 Monterey

1962 Comet

1960 Comet 4-door sedan

1961 Colony Park wagon

1961 Comet 2-door sedan

1962 Monterey 2-door sedan

1962 Meteor 2-door sedan

1963 Comet Custom hardtop coupe

1964 Montclair Marauder hardtop sedan

1964 Comet Cyclone hardtop coupe

MERCURY

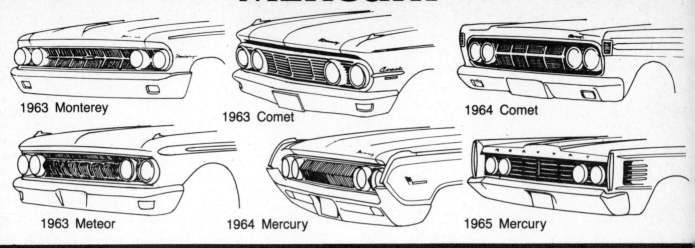

1963 Monterey   1963 Comet   1964 Comet

1963 Meteor   1964 Mercury   1965 Mercury

1965 Comet Cyclone hardtop coupe

1967 Cougar hardtop coupe

1965 Park Lane Breezeway sedan

1968 Montego MX wagon

1966 S-55 convertible

1968 Cougar hardtop coupe

1967 Cougar hardtop coupe

1968 Park Lane Brougham hardtop sedan

MERCURY

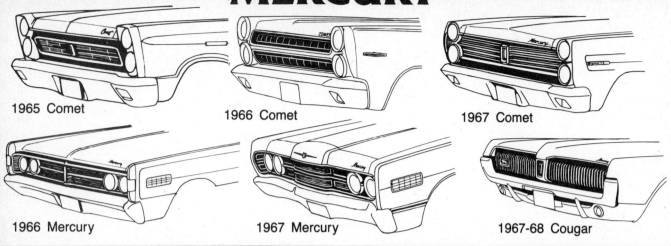

1965 Comet   1966 Comet   1967 Comet

1966 Mercury   1967 Mercury   1967-68 Cougar

1968 Montego MX hardtop coupe

1968 Cougar XR-7 hardtop coupe

1968 Cyclone GT fastback hardtop coupe

1968 Montego MX convertible

1969 Marquis Brougham hardtop sedan

1969 Cyclone CJ fastback hardtop coupe

1969 Montego hardtop coupe

1969 Cyclone Spoiler Dan Gurney fastback hardtop coupe

MERCURY

1968 Mercury

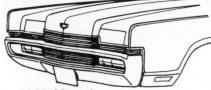
1969 Marquis

1969 Comet, Montego, Cyclone

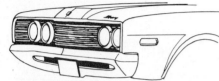
1968 Comet, Montego, Cyclone

1969 Monterey

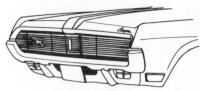
1969 Cougar

1969 Marquis Colony Park wagon

1970 Marauder X-100 hardtop coupe

1969 Monterey hardtop coupe

1970 Marquis Brougham hardtop sedan

1970 Cougar XR-7 convertible

1971 Montego MX Brougham hardtop sedan

1970 Montego MX Brougham hardtop sedan

1971 Monterey hardtop coupe

MERCURY

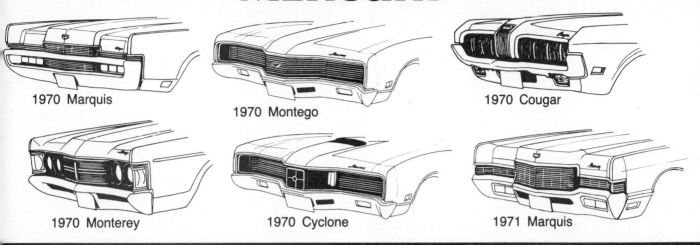

1970 Marquis   1970 Montego   1970 Cougar

1970 Monterey   1970 Cyclone   1971 Marquis

1971 Marquis Brougham hardtop sedan

1971 Cougar XR-7 hardtop coupe

1971 Comet 2-door sedan

1971 Comet 4-door sedan

1972 Montego MX Villager wagon

1972 Marquis Brougham hardtop sedan

1972 Monterey Custom hardtop coupe

1972 Comet 2-door sedan

MERCURY

1971 Monterey   1971 Cyclone   1971-72 Cougar

1971 Montego   1971-72 Comet   1972 Marquis

1972 Comet GT 2-door sedan

1973 Montego MX Brougham hardtop coupe

1973 Monterey 4-door pillared hardtop

1973 Marquis Brougham hardtop sedan

1973 Cougar XR-7 hardtop coupe

1973 Comet 2-door sedan

1974 Montego MX Villager wagon

1974 Monterey hardtop coupe

MERCURY

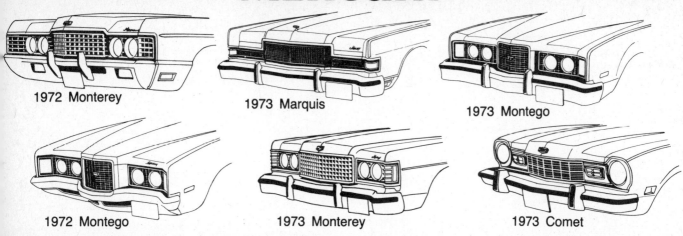

1972 Monterey   1973 Marquis   1973 Montego

1972 Montego   1973 Monterey   1973 Comet

1974 Marquis Colony Park wagon

1974 Marquis Brougham 4-door pillared hardtop

1974 Cougar XR-7 hardtop coupe

1974 Comet Custom 2-door sedan

1974 Montego MX Brougham 4-door pillared hardtop

1975 Montego MX Brougham 4-door pillared hardtop

1975 Grand Marquis 4-door pillared hardtop

1975 Cougar XR-7 hardtop coupe

MERCURY

1973 Cougar   1974 Monterey   1974-75 Comet

1974 Marquis   1974 Montego   1974 Cougar

1975 Comet 4-door sedan

1976 Monarch Ghia 2-door sedan

1975 Bobcat Villager wagon

1976 Marquis Brougham hardtop coupe

1975 Bobcat Runabout hatchback sedan

1976 Cougar XR-7 hardtop coupe

1976 Montego MX Brougham hardtop coupe

1976 Comet Custom 4-door sedan

MERCURY

1975-78 Marquis

1975-76 Cougar

1975-77 Monarch

1975-76 Montego

1975-76 Bobcat

1976-77 Comet

1976 Bobcat MPG Runabout hatchback sedan

1977 Cougar Brougham 4-door sedan

1977 Grand Marquis 4-door sedan

1977 Cougar Brougham 4-door sedan

1977 Monarch Ghia 2-door sedan

1977 Comet Custom 2-door sedan

1977 Marquis Colony Park wagon

1977 Bobcat Runabout hatchback sedan

MERCURY

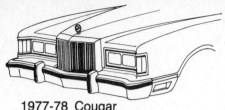

1977-78 Cougar

1977-78 Bobcat

1978-80 Monarch

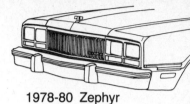

1978-80 Zephyr

1979-80 Marquis

1978 Zephyr Z-7 coupe

1978 Grand Marquis 4-door sedan

1978 Cougar XR-7 hardtop coupe

1978 Bobcat Villager wagon

1979 Zephyr 4-door sedan

1979 Monarch Ghia 4-door sedan

1979 Marquis Colony Park wagon

1979 Marquis Brougham 2-door sedan

MERCURY

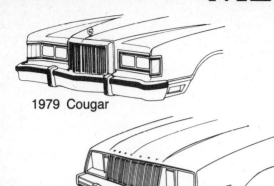

1979 Cougar

1979-80 Capri

1979-80 Bobcat

1980 Cougar XR-7

1979 Capri hatchback coupe

1980 Cougar XR-7 coupe

1979 Cougar XR-7 hardtop coupe

1980 Zephyr Z-7 Turbo coupe (prototype)

1979 Bobcat sedan and Runabout sedan

1980 Monarch Ghia 2-door sedan

1980 Bobcat Sports hatchback sedan

1980 Grand Marquis 4-door sedan

NASH & METROPOLITAN

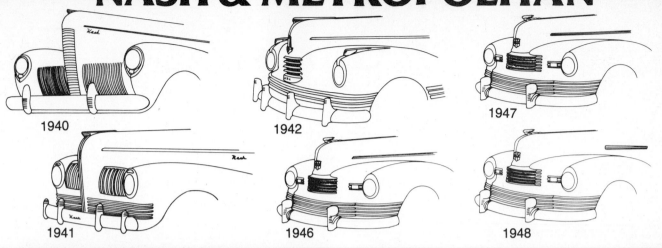

1940 1942 1947

1941 1946 1948

1940 Ambassador Eight cabriolet (custom body)

1940 Ambassador Eight 4-door fastback sedan

1940 Ambassador Eight All-Purpose cabriolet

1941 Ambassador Six 4-door trunkback sedan

1941 Ambassador Eight All-Purpose cabriolet

1942 600 4-door trunkback sedan

1946 Ambassador Suburban 4-door fastback sedan

NASH & METROPOLITAN

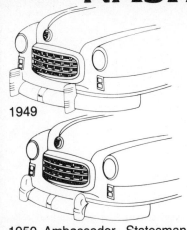

1949

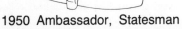

1950 Ambassador, Statesman

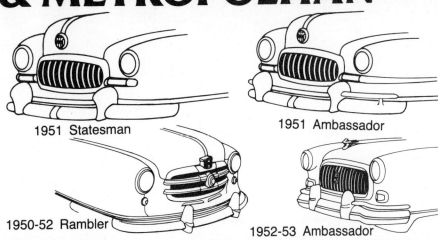

1951 Statesman

1951 Ambassador

1950-52 Rambler

1952-53 Ambassador

1947 Ambassador 4-door trunkback sedan

1948 Ambassador Super 4-door trunkback sedan

1950 Rambler Custom Landau convertible

1949 Ambassador Super 4-door sedan

1952 Statesman Super 2-door sedan

1952 Rambler Greenbrier Suburban wagon

NASH & METROPOLITAN

1952-53
Statesman

1954 Ambassador,
Statesman

1955 Ambassador, Statesman

1953-54
Rambler

1954-56
Metropolitan

1955 Rambler

1953 Ambassador Custom Country Club hardtop coupe

1954 Metropolitan Series 54 coupe

1954 Rambler Greenbrier Suburban wagon

1954 Metropolitan Series 54 convertible

1955 Ambassador Eight Custom 4-door sedan

1955 Ambassador Eight Custom 4-door sedan

1956 Rambler Super 4-door sedan

NASH & METROPOLITAN

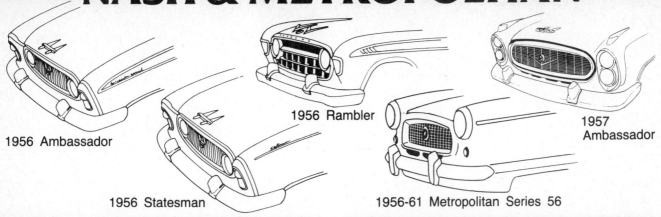

1956 Ambassador

1956 Rambler

1957 Ambassador

1956 Statesman

1956-61 Metropolitan Series 56

1956 Rambler Custom hardtop sedan

1957 Ambassador Super Country Club hardtop coupe

1956 Rambler Custom Cross Country hardtop wagon

1957 Ambassador Custom Country Club hardtop coupe

1956 Ambassador Eight Custom 4-door sedan

1957 Metropolitan 1500 Series 56 convertible

1957 Ambassador Custom 4-door sedan

1957 Metropolitan Series 56 coupe

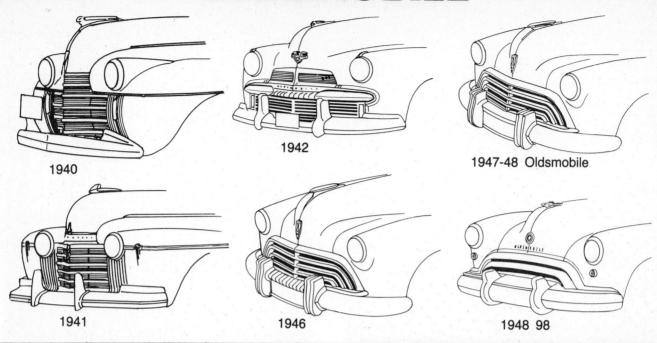

1940

1942

1947-48 Oldsmobile

1941

1946

1948 98

1940 Series 60 club coupe

1940 Series 60 wagon

1940 Series 70 convertible coupe

1941 Special Eight convertible coupe

1940 Series 90 4-door sedan

1941 Special Six 2-door sedan

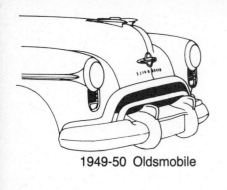

1949-50 Oldsmobile

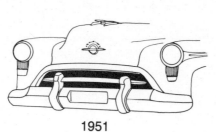

1951

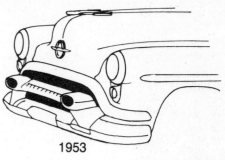

1953

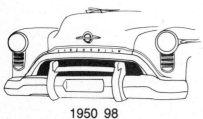

1950 98

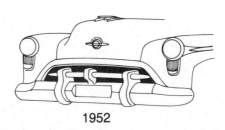

1952

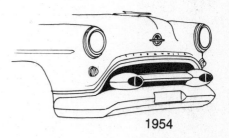

1954

1941 Dynamic Cruiser Six 4-door sedan

1942 Seventy-Eight 4-door sedan

1941 Dynamic Cruiser Eight club coupe

1942 Sixty-Eight club sedan

1942 Ninety-Eight convertible coupe

1942 Sixty-Eight wagon

OLDSMOBILE

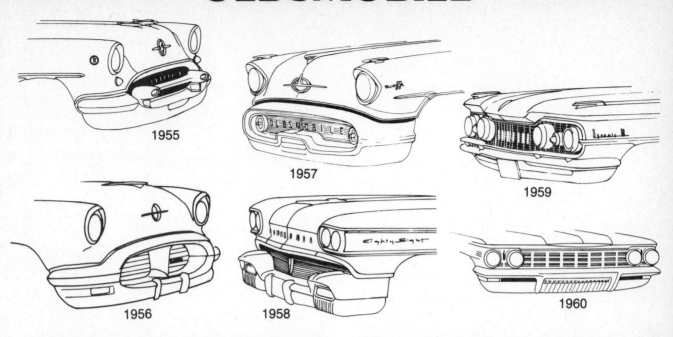

1955   1957   1959

1956   1958   1960

1946 Special 66 convertible

1947 Dynamic Cruiser 76 club sedan

1948 Futuramic 98 convertible

1948 Futuramic 98 4-door sedan

1949 Futuramic 98 Holiday hardtop coupe

1950 Futuramic 88 Deluxe 4-door sedan

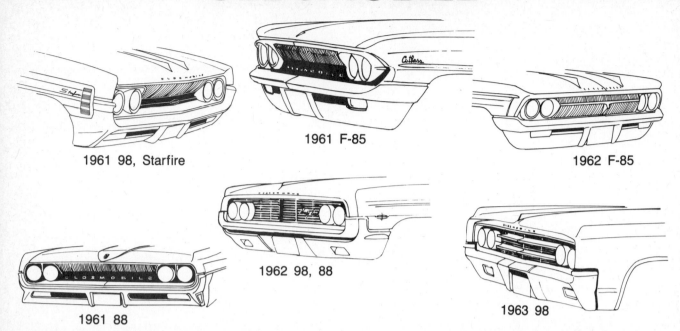

1961 98, Starfire

1961 F-85

1962 F-85

1961 88

1962 98, 88

1963 98

1950 Futuramic 88 Deluxe convertible

1951 Ninety-Eight Holiday hardtop coupe

1950 Futuramic 88 Holiday hardtop coupe

1951 Series 88 2-door sedan

1951 Super 88 convertible

1952 Series 88 Deluxe 2-door sedan

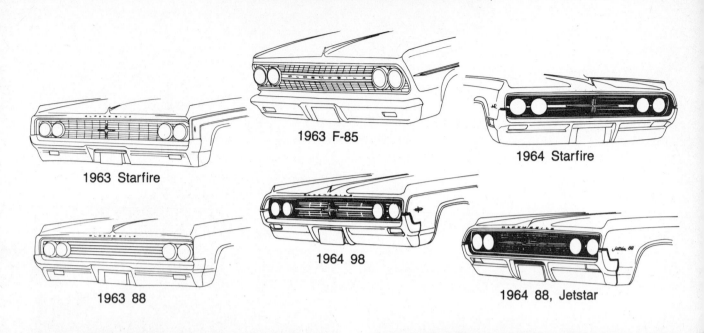

1963 Starfire

1963 F-85

1964 Starfire

1963 88

1964 98

1964 88, Jetstar

1954 Series 88 4-door sedan

1956 Series 88 Holiday hardtop coupe

1955 Ninety-Eight Starfire convertible

1957 Starfire 98 convertible

1955 Ninety-Eight Holiday hardtop sedan

1957 Starfire 98 Holiday hardtop coupe

OLDSMOBILE

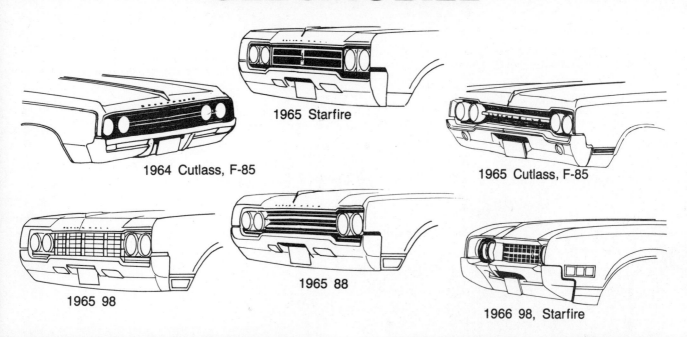

1965 Starfire

1964 Cutlass, F-85

1965 Cutlass, F-85

1965 98

1965 88

1966 98, Starfire

1957 Golden Rocket 88 Holiday hardtop sedan

1957 Golden Rocket Super 88 convertible

1957 Golden Rocket 88 Fiesta hardtop wagon

1958 Dynamic 88 Holiday hardtop coupe

1959 Super 88 Fiesta wagon

1959 Dynamic 88 Sceni-Coupe hardtop

OLDSMOBILE

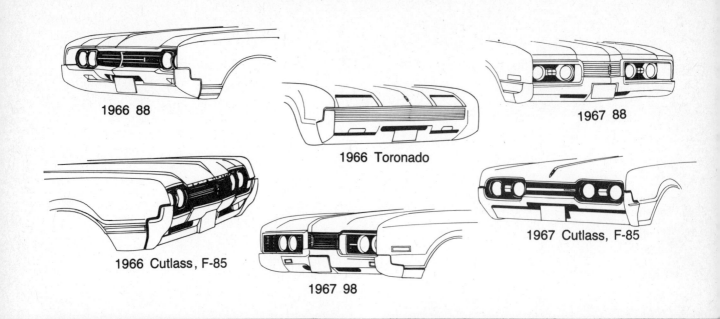

1966 88

1966 Toronado

1967 88

1966 Cutlass, F-85

1967 98

1967 Cutlass, F-85

1960 Ninety-Eight Celebrity sedan

1961 Ninety-Eight Sport Sedan

1960 Super 88 Sceni-Coupe hardtop

1961 Super 88 convertible

1960 Super 88 convertible

1962 F-85 Deluxe Jetfire hardtop coupe

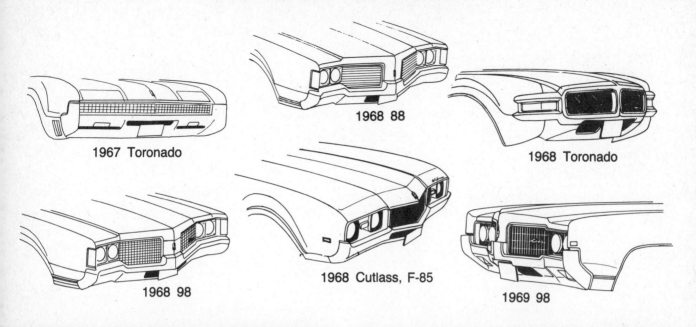

1967 Toronado

1968 88

1968 Toronado

1968 98

1968 Cutlass, F-85

1969 98

1963 Starfire hardtop coupe

1965 Delta 88 Holiday hardtop sedan

1964 Jetstar 88 Celebrity sedan

1965 Ninety-Eight Luxury Sedan

1964 Cutlass Holiday hardtop coupe

1966 Cutlass 4-4-2 Holiday hardtop coupe

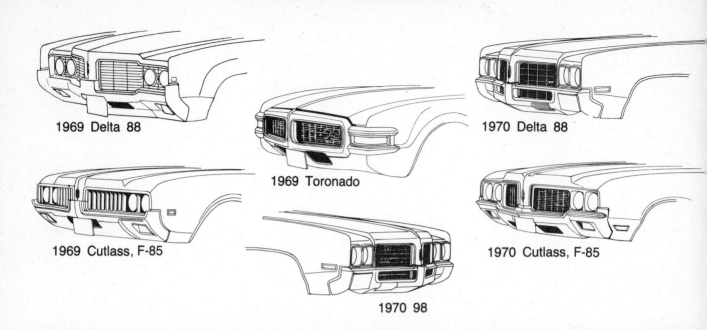

1969 Delta 88

1969 Toronado

1970 Delta 88

1969 Cutlass, F-85

1970 Cutlass, F-85

1970 98

1967 Toronado Deluxe hardtop coupe

1967 4-4-2 Holiday hardtop coupe

1967 Cutlass wagon

OLDSMOBILE

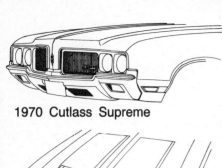

1970 Cutlass Supreme

1970 4-4-2

1970 Toronado

1971 98

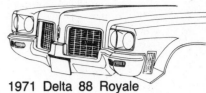

1971 Delta 88 Royale

1971 Delta 88

1967 Delta 88 Custom Holiday hardtop sedan

1967 Ninety-Eight Luxury Sedan

1967 Delta 88 Custom Holiday hardtop coupe

1967 Ninety-Eight Holiday hardtop coupe

1968 Ninety-Eight convertible

1968 Delmont 88 Holiday hardtop sedan

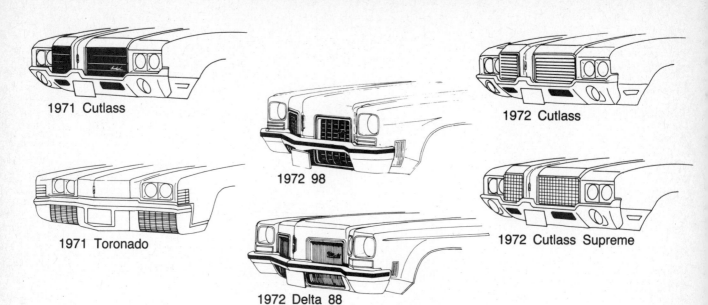

1971 Cutlass

1972 98

1972 Cutlass

1971 Toronado

1972 Cutlass Supreme

1972 Delta 88

1968 Delta 88 Custom Holiday hardtop coupe

1968 Cutlass "S" Holiday hardtop coupe

1968 Toronado Custom hardtop coupe

1968 Vista Cruiser Custom wagon

1968 4-4-2 Holiday hardtop coupe

1969 Ninety-Eight Luxury hardtop sedan

OLDSMOBILE

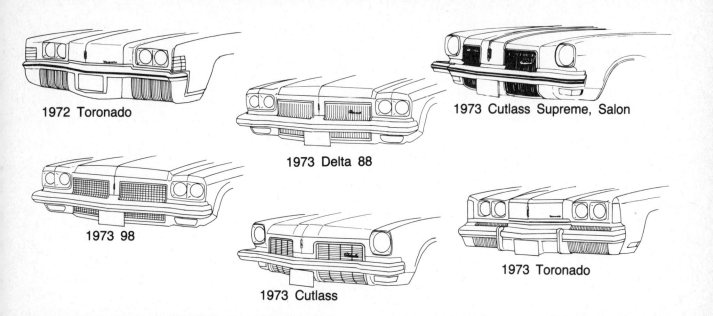

1972 Toronado

1973 Delta 88

1973 Cutlass Supreme, Salon

1973 98

1973 Cutlass

1973 Toronado

1969 Toronado Custom hardtop coupe

1969 Delta 88 Royale Holiday hardtop coupe

1969 Delta 88 Custom Holiday hardtop sedan

1969 Vista Cruiser wagon

1969 Cutlass Supreme Holiday hardtop sedan

1969 4-4-2 Holiday hardtop coupe

Specially equipped 4-4-2s prepared by Hurst Performance Products were marketed by Oldsmobile in 1968 and 1969 as the Hurst/Olds.

1973 Omega

1974 Delta 88

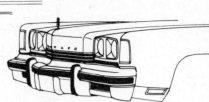

1974 Toronado

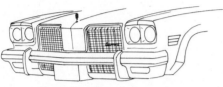

1974 98

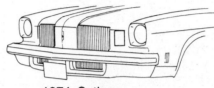

1974 Cutlass

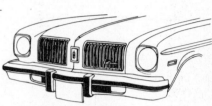

1974 Omega

1970 Toronado Custom hardtop coupe

1970 Cutlass Supreme Holiday hardtop coupe

1970 Delta 88 Custom Holiday hardtop sedan

1970 Ninety-Eight Holiday Coupe

1971 Cutlass "S" hardtop coupe

1971 Delta 88 Custom hardtop coupe

1971 Ninety-Eight hardtop coupe

1971 Toronado hardtop coupe

OLDSMOBILE

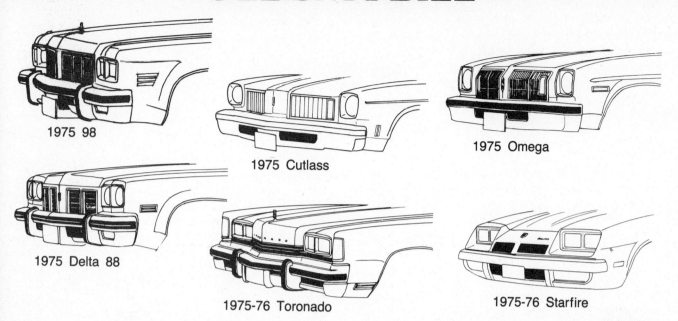

1975 98

1975 Cutlass

1975 Omega

1975 Delta 88

1975-76 Toronado

1975-76 Starfire

1972 Cutlass Cruiser wagon

1973 Cutlass Supreme Colonnade coupe

1972 Delta 88 Royale hardtop coupe

1973 Cutlass "S" Colonnade coupe

1972 Toronado hardtop coupe

1973 Ninety-Eight Regency hardtop coupe

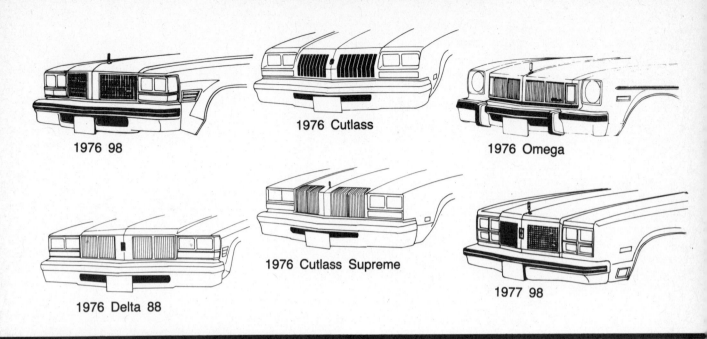

1976 98

1976 Cutlass

1976 Omega

1976 Delta 88

1976 Cutlass Supreme

1977 98

1973 Omega hatchback coupe

1974 Delta 88 Town Sedan

1973 Toronado Brougham hardtop coupe

1974 Toronado Brougham coupe

1974 Ninety-Eight Regency hardtop coupe

1975 Cutlass "S" Colonnade hardtop coupe

OLDSMOBILE

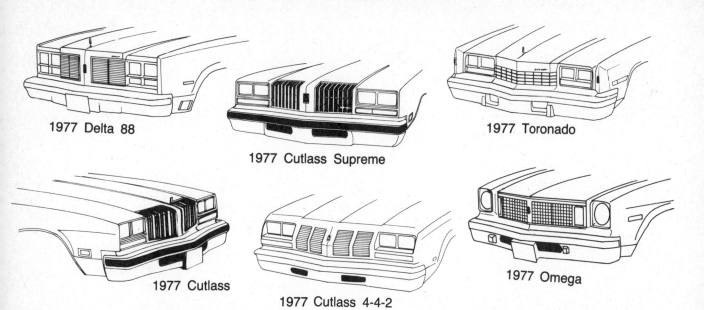

1977 Delta 88

1977 Cutlass Supreme

1977 Toronado

1977 Cutlass

1977 Cutlass 4-4-2

1977 Omega

1975 Omega Salon 4-door sedan

1976 Vista Cruiser wagon

1975 Starfire hatchback coupe

1976 Omega Brougham Landau coupe

1976 Cutlass "S" Colonnade hardtop sedan

1976 Toronado coupe

OLDSMOBILE

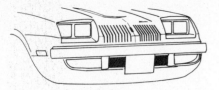
1977-78 Starfire

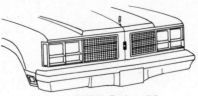
1978 Delta 88

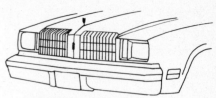
1978 Cutlass Calais

1978 98

1978 Cutlass Supreme

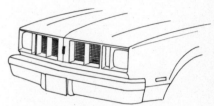
1978 Cutlass Salon, 4-4-2

1977 Cutlass 4-4-2 coupe

1977 Omega coupe

1977 Ninety-Eight Luxury Coupe

1977 Starfire SX hatchback coupe

1977 Delta 88 Royale Town Sedan

1977 Toronado XSR coupe

OLDSMOBILE

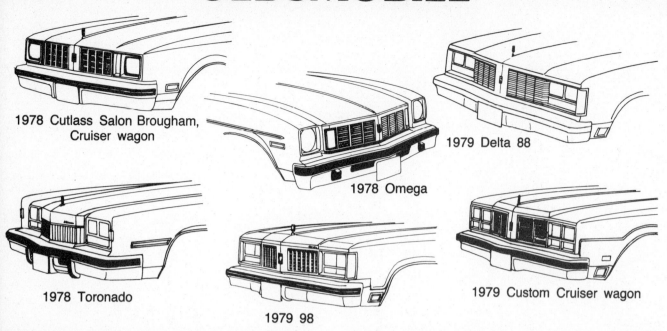

1978 Cutlass Salon Brougham,
Cruiser wagon

1978 Omega

1979 Delta 88

1978 Toronado

1979 98

1979 Custom Cruiser wagon

1978 Cutlass Supreme coupe

1978 Custom Cruiser wagon

1978 Cutlass Salon coupe

1979 Cutlass Calais coupe

1978 Delta 88 coupe

1979 Cutlass Cruiser Brougham Diesel wagon

OLDSMOBILE

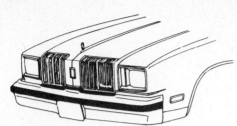
1979 Cutlass Supreme

1979 Cutlass Salon

1979 Toronado

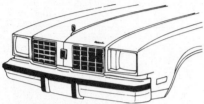
1979 Cutlass Calais

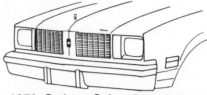
1979 Cutlass Salon Brougham,
Cutlass Cruiser wagon

1979 Omega

1979 Delta 88 Royale sedan

1979 Starfire Firenza hatchback coupe

1979 Toronado Diesel coupe

1980 Delta 88 Royale Brougham sedan

1979 Toronado Diesel coupe

1980 Custom Cruiser wagon

OLDSMOBILE

1979 Starfire

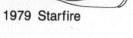

1980 Cutlass Supreme

1980 Toronado

1980 Delta 88

1980 Cutlass Calais, Brougham

1980 Omega

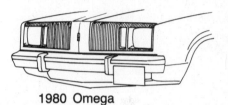

1980 98

1980 Cutlass Salon

1980 Starfire

1980 Cutlass Supreme Brougham coupe

1980 Toronado Brougham Diesel coupe

1980 Omega Brougham sedan

1980 Omega coupe

PACKARD & CLIPPER

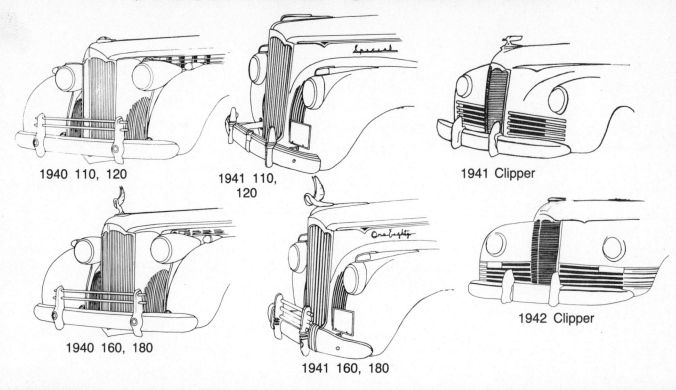

1940 110, 120

1941 110, 120

1941 Clipper

1940 160, 180

1941 160, 180

1942 Clipper

1940 Custom Super Eight 180 convertible victoria by Darrin

1940 Custom Super Eight 180 convertible victoria by Darrin

1940 One Ten convertible coupe

1941 Super Eight 160 convertible sedan

1941 Clipper 4-door sedan

1941 One Ten Deluxe 4-door sedan

PACKARD & CLIPPER

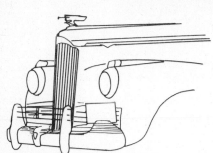

1942 110, 120 convertible and special body models

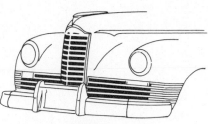

1946-47

1948-49 Super, DeLuxe, Standard

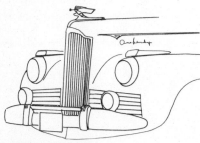

1942 160, 180 special body models

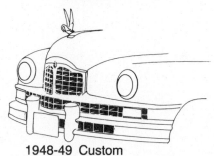

1948-49 Custom

1949-50 Custom, Super DeLuxe

1942 Clipper 120 convertible coupe

1942 Clipper 160 4-door sedan

1942 Clipper 180 convertible victoria by Darrin

1942 Clipper 120 convertible coupe

1942 Clipper 160 4-door touring sedan

1946 Custom Super Clipper 4-door sedan

PACKARD & CLIPPER

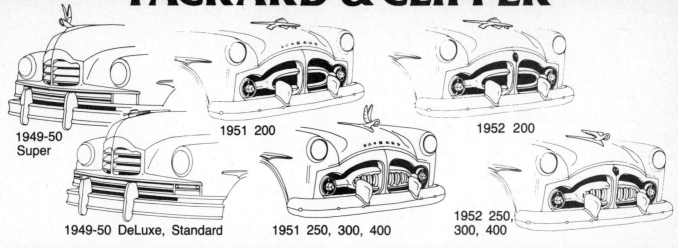

1949-50 Super

1951 200

1952 200

1949-50 DeLuxe, Standard

1951 250, 300, 400

1952 250, 300, 400

1946 Clipper Deluxe Eight club sedan

1947 Custom Super Clipper club sedan

1948 Eight Station Sedan wagon

1948 Custom Eight 4-door sedan

1949-50 Super Eight Deluxe convertible

1951 Patrician 400 sedan

1952 Patrician 400 sedan

1953 convertible (Series 2631)

PACKARD & CLIPPER

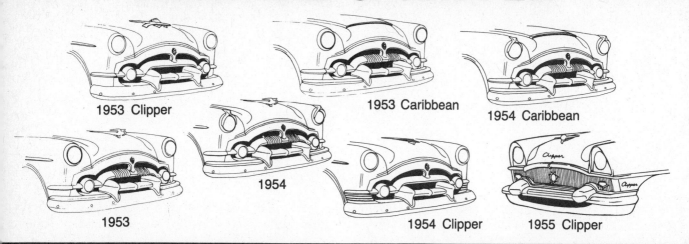

1953 Clipper   1953 Caribbean   1954 Caribbean

1953   1954   1954 Clipper   1955 Clipper

1953 Patrician formal sedan by Derham

1954 Clipper Super Panama hardtop coupe

1954 Patrician sedan

1955 Four Hundred hardtop coupe

1955 Clipper Super Panama hardtop coupe

1956 Clipper Custom Constellation hardtop coupe

1956 Four Hundred hardtop coupe

1956 Caribbean hardtop coupe

PACKARD & CLIPPER

1955 Caribbean, Patrician, 400

1956 Caribbean

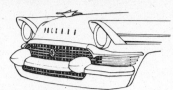

1957 Clipper

1956 Clipper

1956 Patrician, 400

1958 sedan,
hardtop, wagon

1958 Hawk

1956 Caribbean hardtop coupe

1957 Clipper Country Sedan wagon

1957 Clipper Town Sedan

1958 Hawk hardtop coupe

1958 wagon

PLYMOUTH

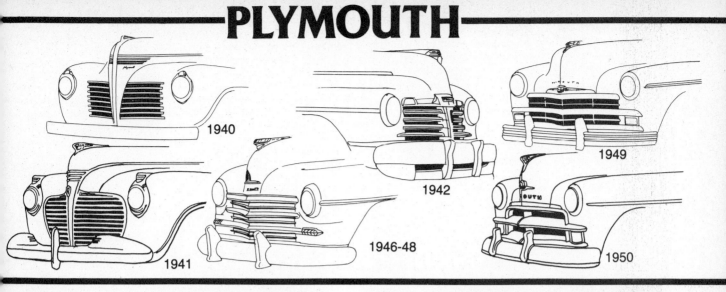

1940

1941

1942

1946-48

1949

1950

1940 DeLuxe 4-door sedan

1942 Special DeLuxe convertible coupe

1941 DeLuxe club coupe

1946-48 DeLuxe club coupe

1949 Special DeLuxe convertible

PLYMOUTH

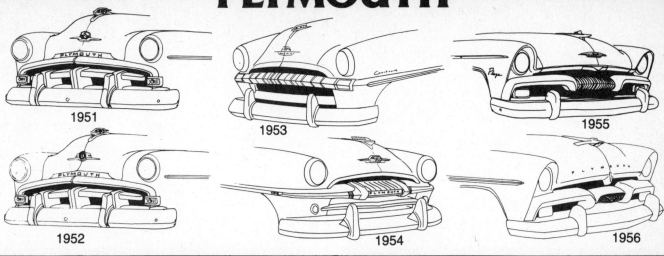

1951
1952
1953
1954
1955
1956

1949 DeLuxe Suburban 2-door wagon

1949 Special DeLuxe club coupe

1951 Cranbrook Belvedere hardtop coupe

1950 DeLuxe business coupe

1953 Cranbrook club coupe

1954 Belvedere Sport Coupe hardtop

1954 Belvedere 4-door sedan

PLYMOUTH

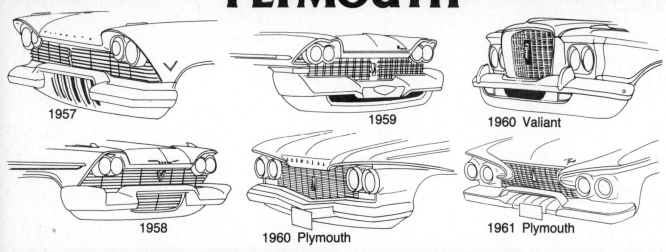

1957   1959   1960 Valiant

1958   1960 Plymouth   1961 Plymouth

1955 Belvedere Sport Coupe hardtop

1955 Savoy 4-door sedan

1955 Belvedere Suburban 4-door wagon

1956 Plaza club sedan

1956 Sport Suburban wagon

1956 Belvedere convertible

1956 Fury hardtop coupe

1957 Fury hardtop coupe

PLYMOUTH

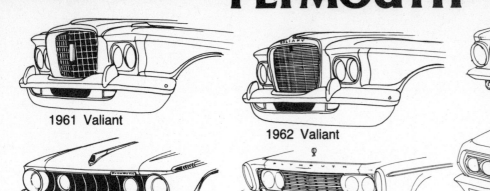

1961 Valiant

1962 Valiant

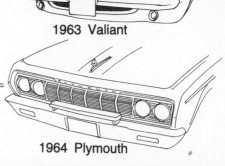

1963 Valiant

1962 Plymouth

1963 Plymouth

1964 Plymouth

1957 Savoy 4-door sedan

1958 Sport Suburban wagon

1957 Belvedere Sport Sedan hardtop

1958 Belvedere Sport Sedan hardtop

1957 Custom Suburban 2-door wagon

1959 Belvedere convertible

1958 Fury hardtop coupe

1960 Fury hardtop sedan

PLYMOUTH

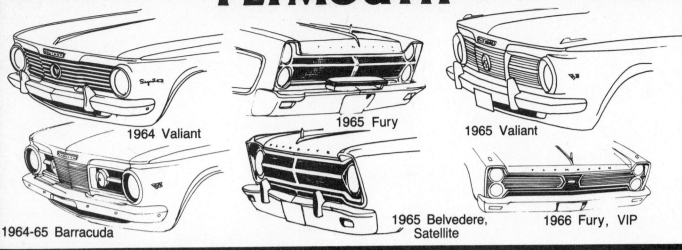

1964 Valiant

1965 Fury

1965 Valiant

1964-65 Barracuda

1965 Belvedere, Satellite

1966 Fury, VIP

1960 Fury convertible

1960 Valiant V200 4-door sedan

1961 Fury hardtop coupe

1961 Fury convertible

1962 Sport Fury convertible

1962 Savoy 2-door sedan

1962 Valiant V200 4-door sedan

1962 Valiant V200 4-door sedan

PLYMOUTH

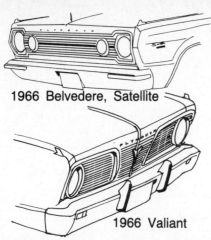
1966 Belvedere, Satellite

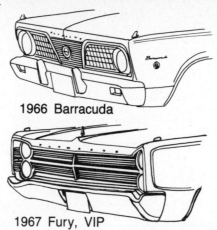
1966 Barracuda

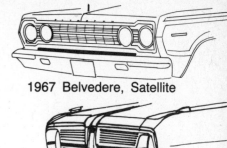
1967 Belvedere, Satellite

1966 Valiant

1967 Fury, VIP

1967 Valiant

1963 Sport Fury hardtop coupe

1963 Fury hardtop sedan

1963 Valiant Signet 200 hardtop coupe

1965 Valiant Signet convertible

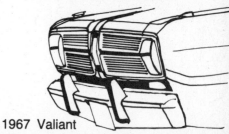
1965 Fury III wagon

1966 Barracuda Formula S fastback hardtop coupe

1966 Barracuda Formula S fastback hardtop coupe

1966 Satellite hardtop coupe

PLYMOUTH

1967 Barracuda

1968 Belvedere, Sport Satellite

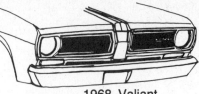

1968 Valiant

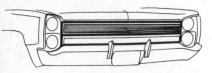

1968 Fury, VIP

1968 Road Runner, Satellite

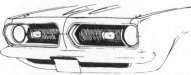

1968 Barracuda

1967 VIP hardtop sedan

1967 Barracuda Formula S fastback hardtop coupe

1967 Sport Fury convertible

1967 Valiant Signet 4-door sedan

1967 Belvedere II 4-door sedan

1968 Sport Fury fastback hardtop coupe

1967 Satellite 426 hardtop coupe

1968 Barracuda Formula S fastback hardtop coupe

PLYMOUTH

1969 Fury

1969 Road Runner

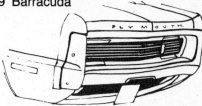
1969 Barracuda

1969 Satellite, Belvedere

1969 Valiant

1970 Gran Fury, Sport Fury

1968 Barracuda Formula S fastback hardtop coupe

1968 Barracuda hardtop coupe

1968 Sport Satellite wagon

1969 Sport Suburban wagon

1968 GTX convertible

1969 Valiant Signet 4-door sedan

1969 Road Runner hardtop coupe

1969 GTX hardtop coupe

PLYMOUTH

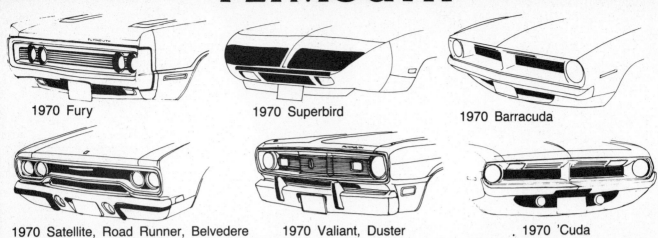

1970 Fury   1970 Superbird   1970 Barracuda

1970 Satellite, Road Runner, Belvedere   1970 Valiant, Duster   1970 'Cuda

1969 Road Runner convertible

1969 Barracuda fastback hardtop coupe

1970 Road Runner coupe

1970 Road Runner Superbird hardtop coupe

1970 Sport Fury GT hardtop coupe

1970 Valiant Duster coupe

1971 'Cuda 340 hardtop coupe

1971 Road Runner hardtop coupe

PLYMOUTH

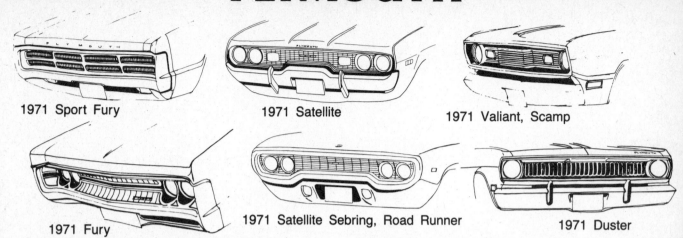

1971 Sport Fury

1971 Satellite

1971 Valiant, Scamp

1971 Fury

1971 Satellite Sebring, Road Runner

1971 Duster

1971 Sport Fury hardtop coupe

1971 Satellite Custom sedan

1971 Duster 340 coupe

1971 Valiant Scamp hardtop coupe

1972 Fury Gran Coupe hardtop

1972 Satellite Sebring Plus hardtop coupe

1973 Barracuda hardtop coupe

1973 Fury Gran Coupe hardtop

PLYMOUTH

1971 Barracuda

1972 Fury

1972 Satellite Sebring

1972 Fury Gran Coupe, Sedan

1972 Satellite

1972 Road Runner

1973 Satellite Sebring Plus hardtop coupe

1973 Road Runner hardtop coupe

1973 Duster coupe

1974 Fury Gran Sedan hardtop

1975 Gran Fury Brougham coupe

1975 Fury Sport hardtop coupe

1975 Duster Custom coupe

PLYMOUTH

1972 Valiant, Duster, Scamp

1973 Fury

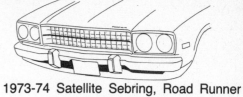

1973-74 Satellite Sebring, Road Runner

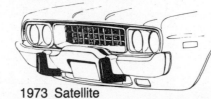

1973 Satellite

1972 Barracuda

1973-74 Valiant, Duster, Scamp

1976 Fury Sport coupe

1976 Gran Fury Brougham coupe

1976 Volaré Premier sedan

1976 Volaré Premier coupe

1976 Feather Duster coupe

1977 Gran Fury Brougham coupe

1977 Gran Fury Brougham coupe

1977 Fury Salon sedan

PLYMOUTH

1973-74 Barracuda

1974 Satellite

1975 Gran Fury Custom

1974 Fury

1975-77 Gran Fury Brougham

1975 Fury

1977 Fury Sport coupe

1977 Volaré Road Runner coupe

1977 Volaré Custom coupe

1977 Volaré Premier wagon

1978 Horizon hatchback sedan

1978 Horizon hatchback sedan

1978 Fury Sport hardtop coupe

1978 Fury Salon sedan

217

PLYMOUTH

1975-76 Valiant,
Duster, Scamp

1977-78 Fury

1976-77 Volare

1978-80 Horizon

1978 Volaré Premier sedan

1978 Volaré Road Runner coupe

1978 Volaré Premier wagon

1979 Horizon TC3 hatchback coupe

1979 Volaré Road Runner coupe

PLYMOUTH

1978-79 Volare

1979-80 Horizon TC3

1980 Gran Fury

1980 Volare, Duster

1979 Volaré Sport Wagon

1980 Volaré Premier coupe

1980 Gran Fury sedan

1980 Horizon TC3 hatchback coupe

1980 Horizon hatchback sedan

PONTIAC

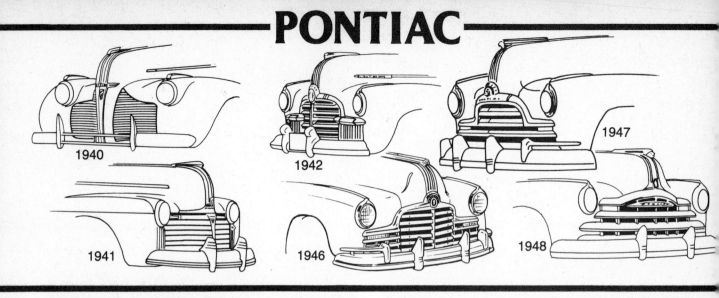

1940

1941

1942

1946

1947

1948

1940 Torpedo Eight sport coupe

1940 Torpedo Eight sport coupe

1940 Torpedo Eight 4-door sedan

1941 Custom Torpedo Eight DeLuxe wagon

1941 Custom Torpedo Eight sedan coupe

PONTIAC

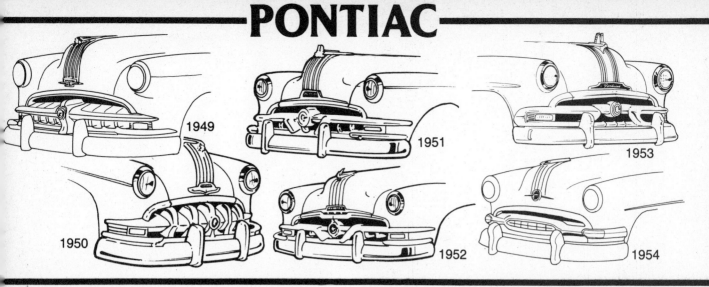

1949
1950
1951
1952
1953
1954

1941 Custom Torpedo Eight 4-door sedan

1941 Custom Torpedo Eight DeLuxe wagon

1942 Torpedo Eight 4-door sedan

1946 Streamliner Eight 4-door sedan

1946 Torpedo Eight convertible

1947 Torpedo Eight 4-door sedan

1948 Torpedo Eight coupe sedan

1949 Streamliner Eight DeLuxe coupe sedan

PONTIAC

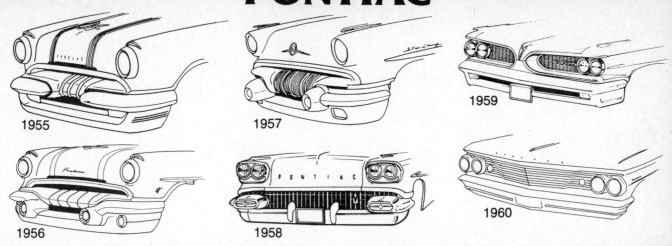

1955

1957

1959

1956

1958

1960

1950 Chieftain Eight Super Catalina hardtop coupe

1951 Chieftain Eight DeLuxe 4-door sedan

1952 Chieftain Eight DeLuxe 4-door sedan

1953 Chieftain Six 4-door sedan

1953 Chieftain Eight Custom Catalina hardtop coupe

1954 Star Chief Custom Catalina hardtop coupe

1954 Chieftain Eight DeLuxe 4-door sedan

1955 Star Chief convertible

PONTIAC

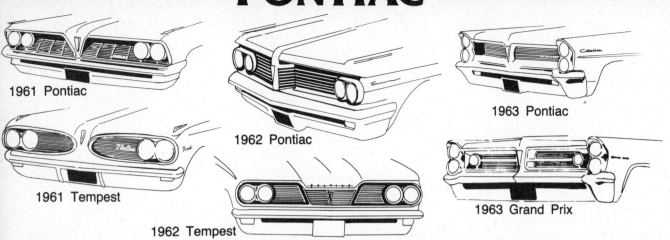

1961 Pontiac

1961 Tempest

1962 Pontiac

1962 Tempest

1963 Pontiac

1963 Grand Prix

1955 Star Chief Custom Catalina hardtop coupe

1956 Star Chief Custom Catalina hardtop sedan

1957 Star Chief Custom Catalina hardtop coupe

1956 Safari hardtop wagon

1957 Star Chief convertible

PONTIAC

1963 Tempest

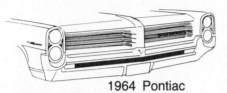

1964 Grand Prix

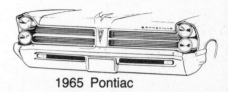

1964 GTO

1964 Pontiac

1964 Tempest

1965 Pontiac

1957 Super Chief 4-door sedan

1957 Bonneville convertible

1957 Super Chief Safari wagon

1958 Star Chief Custom Catalina hardtop sedan

1959 Catalina Vista hardtop sedan

PONTIAC

1965 Grand Prix

1965 GTO

1966 Grand Prix

1965 Tempest

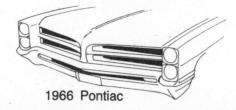

1966 Pontiac

1966 Tempest, LeMans

1959 Catalina hardtop coupe

1960 Catalina 2-door sedan

1960 Catalina Vista hardtop sedan

1960 Bonneville Vista hardtop sedan

1961 Tempest LeMans sport coupe (prototype)

1962 Grand Prix hardtop coupe

1962 Star Chief 4-door sedan

1964 Tempest GTO hardtop coupe

225

PONTIAC

1966 GTO

1967 Grand Prix

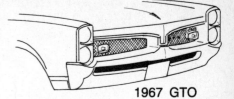
1967 GTO

1967 Pontiac

1967 Tempest, LeMans

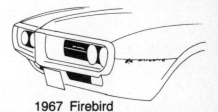
1967 Firebird

1966 Tempest GTO convertible

1966 LeMans sport coupe

1967 Tempest GTO hardtop coupe

1967 Bonneville Brougham hardtop sedan

1967 Catalina Ventura hardtop coupe

1967 Catalina 4-door sedan

1967 Firebird hardtop coupe

1968 Firebird hardtop coupe

PONTIAC

1968 Pontiac

1968 Tempest, LeMans

1969 Bonneville

1968 Grand Prix

1968 GTO

1968 Firebird

1969 Catalina, Ventura, Executive

1968 Firebird convertible

1968 Grand Prix hardtop coupe

1968 Catalina hardtop coupe

1968 LeMans hardtop sedan

1968 LeMans hardtop sedan

1968 Tempest Safari wagon

1968 Executive hardtop sedan

1968 Grand Prix hardtop coupe

PONTIAC

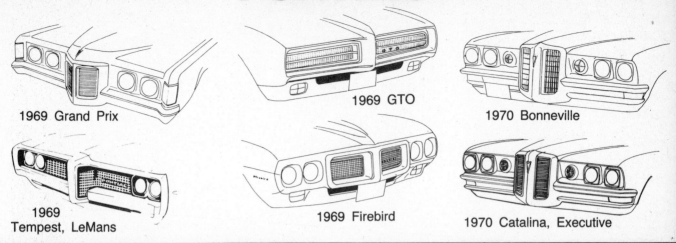

1969 Grand Prix

1969 GTO

1970 Bonneville

1969 Tempest, LeMans

1969 Firebird

1970 Catalina, Executive

1969 Bonneville convertible

1969 Tempest GTO hardtop coupe

1969 Grand Prix Model J hardtop coupe

1969 Firebird hardtop coupe

1969 Catalina hardtop coupe

1970 Grand Prix SJ hardtop coupe

1969 Firebird convertible

1970 LeMans hardtop sedan

PONTIAC

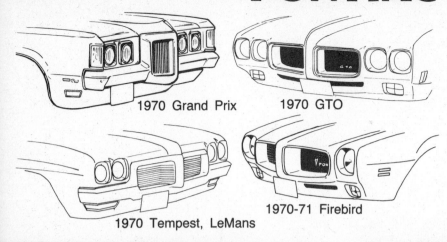

1970 Grand Prix   1970 GTO

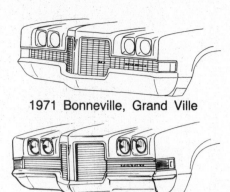

1971 Bonneville, Grand Ville

1970 Tempest, LeMans   1970-71 Firebird

1971 Catalina

1970 Firebird Formula 400 coupe

1972 Firebird Formula 455 coupe

1970 Bonneville Brougham hardtop sedan

1972 Safari wagon

1971 LeMans T-37 hardtop coupe

1972 Luxury LeMans hardtop coupe

1971 GTO convertible

1972 Grand Prix Model SJ hardtop coupe

PONTIAC

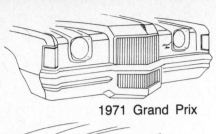

1971 Grand Prix

1971 GTO

1972 Bonneville, Grand Ville

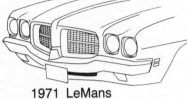

1971 LeMans

1971-72 Ventura II

1972 Catalina

1972 GTO hardtop coupe

1972 Grand Ville hardtop sedan

1972 Catalina hardtop coupe

1973 Ventura Custom 4-door sedan

1973 LeMans Sport Coupe

1973 LeMans GTO Sport Coupe

1973 Ventura Sprint coupe

1973 Grand Am Colonnade hardtop coupe

PONTIAC

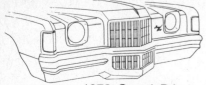

1972 Grand Prix

1972 Luxury LeMans

1972 Firebird

1972 LeMans

1972 GTO

1973 Bonneville, Grand Ville

1973 Grand Prix coupe

1973 Catalina hardtop coupe

1973 Firebird Esprit coupe

1974 Ventura GTO 2-door sedan

1974 Ventura Custom 4-door sedan

1974 Grand Am Colonnade hardtop coupe

1974 LeMans GT Colonnade hardtop coupe

1974 Grand Prix coupe

PONTIAC

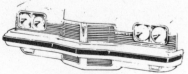

1973 Catalina

1973 LeMans, GTO

1973 Grand Am

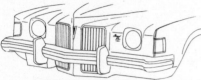

1973 Grand Prix

1973 Luxury LeMans

1973 Firebird

1974 Grand Ville hardtop sedan

1974 Firebird Trans Am coupe

1974 Catalina hardtop coupe

1975 Grand LeMans Safari wagon

1974 Catalina hardtop sedan

1975 Grand LeMans Colonnade hardtop coupe

1974 Firebird Esprit coupe

1975 Grand Am Colonnade hardtop coupe

PONTIAC

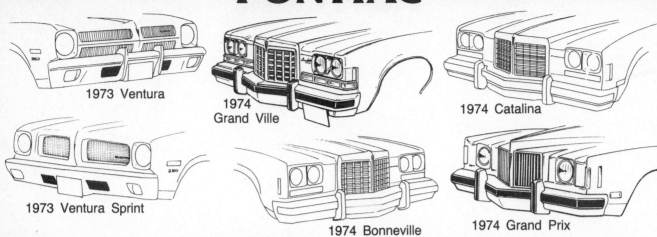

1973 Ventura

1974 Grand Ville

1974 Catalina

1973 Ventura Sprint

1974 Bonneville

1974 Grand Prix

1975 Grand Prix LJ coupe

1975 Catalina 4-door sedan

1975 Grand Prix coupe

1975 Grand Ville Brougham hardtop sedan

1975 Firebird Trans Am coupe

PONTIAC

1974 LeMans

1974 Grand Am

1974 Ventura

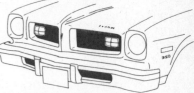

1974 Luxury LeMans

1974 Firebird

1974 Ventura GTO

1975 Astre hatchback coupe

1975 Firebird coupe

1976 Sunbird coupe

1976 Sunbird coupe

1976 Ventura SJ Landau coupe

PONTIAC

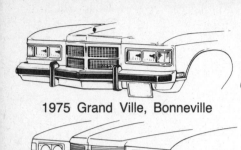

1975 Grand Ville, Bonneville

1975 Grand Prix

1975 LeMans

1975 Catalina

1975 Grand LeMans

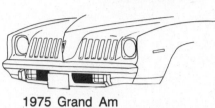

1975 Grand Am

1976 Grand LeMans hardtop coupe

1976 Astre 2-door sedan

1976 Grand Prix coupe

1976 Astre hatchback coupe

1976 Catalina 4-door sedan

1976 Firebird Trans Am coupe

1976 Bonneville hardtop coupe

1976 Firebird Formula coupe

PONTIAC

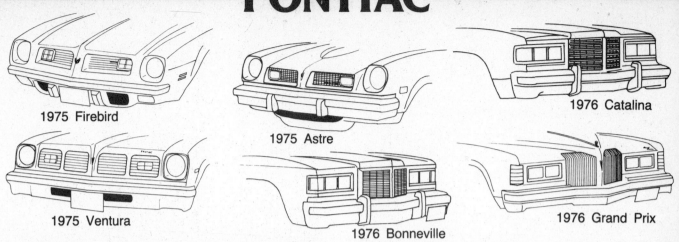

1975 Firebird

1975 Astre

1976 Catalina

1975 Ventura

1976 Bonneville

1976 Grand Prix

1977 Sunbird Formula coupe

1977 Ventura hatchback coupe

1977 LeMans GT hardtop coupe

1977 Sunbird coupe

1977 Astre Safari wagon

PONTIAC

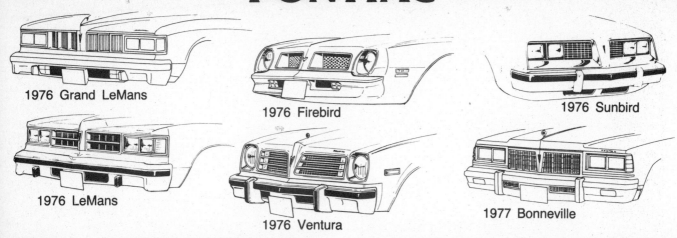

1976 Grand LeMans

1976 Firebird

1976 Sunbird

1976 LeMans

1976 Ventura

1977 Bonneville

1977 Grand LeMans 4-door sedan

1977 Grand Prix SJ coupe

1977 Grand Safari wagon

1977 Catalina 4-door sedan

1977 Catalina Landau coupe

1977 Astre Formula hatchback coupe

1977 Firebird Formula coupe

1977 Firebird Esprit coupe

PONTIAC

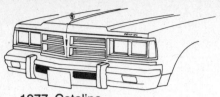

1977 Catalina

1977 Grand Prix

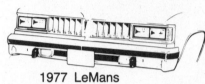

1977 Grand LeMans

1977 LeMans

1977 Firebird

1977 Ventura

1978 Sunbird coupe

1978 Phoenix 4-door sedan

1978 Grand Prix coupe

1978 Grand Prix coupe

1978 Grand Am 4-door sedan

PONTIAC

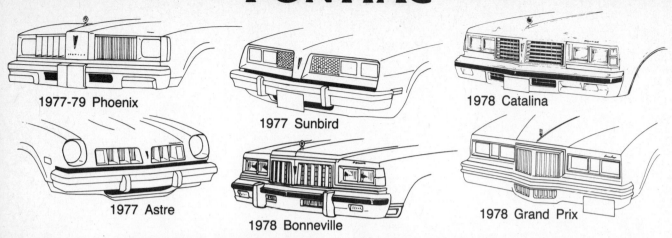

1977-79 Phoenix

1977 Sunbird

1978 Catalina

1977 Astre

1978 Bonneville

1978 Grand Prix

1978 Grand LeMans coupe

1978 Grand LeMans 4-door sedan

1978 Grand Prix coupe

1978 Grand Safari wagon

1978 Bonneville Landau coupe

1978 Catalina 4-door sedan

1978 Firebird Formula coupe

1978 Firebird Special Edition Trans Am coupe

239

PONTIAC

1978 Grand LeMans, LeMans

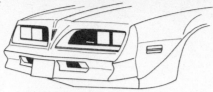
1978 Firebird

1979 Bonneville

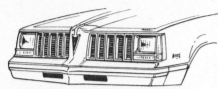
1978-79 Grand Am

1978 Sunbird

1979 Catalina

1979 Grand Prix coupe

1979 Grand Am coupe

1979 Sunbird Safari wagon

1979 Grand LeMans 4-door sedan

1979 Phoenix LJ Landau coupe

1979 Sunbird Formula Sport Hatch coupe

1979 Grand LeMans Safari wagon

1979 Catalina coupe

PONTIAC

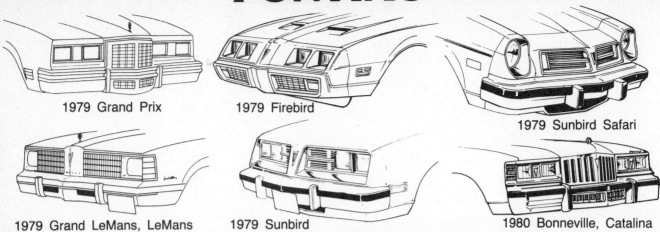

1979 Grand Prix   1979 Firebird   1979 Sunbird Safari

1979 Grand LeMans, LeMans   1979 Sunbird   1980 Bonneville, Catalina

1979 Firebird Special Edition Trans Am

1979 Bonneville Safari wagon

1980 Phoenix SJ coupe

1979 Bonneville 4-door sedan

1980 Phoenix SJ hatchback sedan

241

PONTIAC

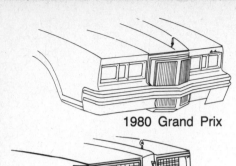

1980 Grand Prix

1980 Grand Am

1980 Phoenix

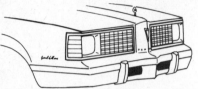

1980 Grand LeMans, LeMans

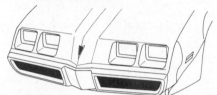

1980 Firebird

1980 Sunbird

1980 Grand LeMans 4-door sedan

1980 Grand Am coupe

1980 Firebird Turbo Trans Am coupe

1980 Grand Prix LJ coupe

RAMBLER

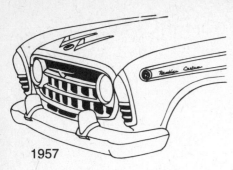

1957

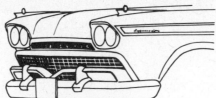

1958 Ambassador

1959 Rebel, Six

1958 Rebel, Six

1958-60 American

1959 Ambassador

1957 Custom Rebel hardtop sedan

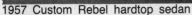

1957 Custom Rebel hardtop sedan

1957 Custom Cross Country hardtop wagon

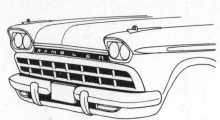

1960 Rebel, Six

1961 Ambassador

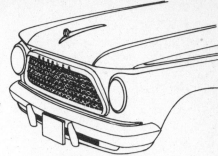

1961 American

1960 Ambassador

1961 Classic

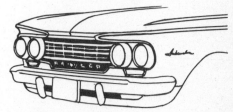

1962 Ambassador

1958 Rebel Custom 4-door sedan

1960 American Super 2-door wagon

1960 American Super 4-door sedan

RAMBLER

1962 Classic

1963 Ambassador

1963 American

1962 American

1963 Classic

1964 Ambassador

1961 Ambassador Custom 4-door sedan

1962 Ambassador 400 4-door sedan

1961 American Custom convertible

1962 Classic Custom 2-door sedan

1962 American Custom 4-door wagon

1963 Ambassador 990 2-door sedan

RAMBLER

1964 Classic

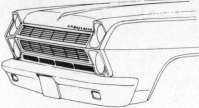
1965 Ambassador

1965 American

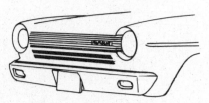
1964 American

1965 Classic

1965 Marlin

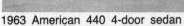
1963 American 440 4-door sedan

1965 Classic 770 convertible

1965 Marlin fastback hardtop coupe

1967 Rebel SST hardtop coupe

1965 American 220 2-door sedan

1967 Rebel SST convertible

RAMBLER

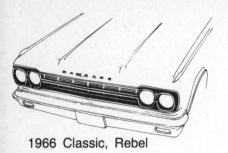

1966 Classic, Rebel

1967 Rebel

1968 American, Rogue

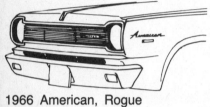

1966 American, Rogue

1967 American, Rogue

1969 American, Rogue

1967 American 440 4-door sedan

1968 American 440 wagon

1967 American 440 4-door sedan

1969 American 440 4-door sedan

1967 American Rogue convertible

1969 American Rogue hardtop coupe

SHELBY

1965-66 GT-350

1968 GT-350, 500, 500 KR

1967 GT-350, 500

1969-70 GT-350, 500

1965 GT-350 fastback coupe

1968 GT-500KR fastback coupe

1968 GT-500 convertible

1968 GT-500KR fastback coupe

1969 GT-500 fastback coupe

1968 GT-500 fastback coupe

1969 GT-500 convertible

STUDEBAKER

1940 Commander, President

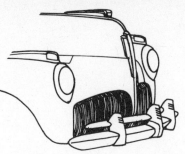

1941 Commander, President

1942 Commander, President

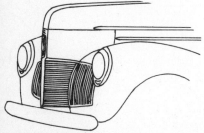

1940 Champion

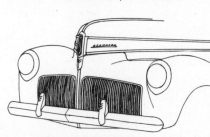

1941 Champion

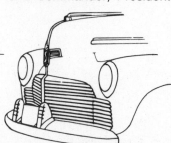

1942 Champion

1940 Commander Custom coupe

1941 Champion Custom Cruising Sedan

1941 President Skyway Land Cruiser sedan

249

STUDEBAKER

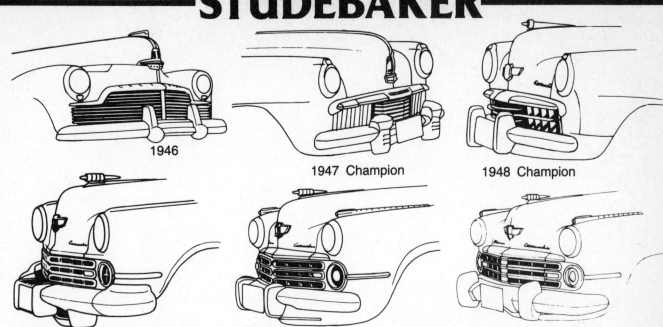

1946

1947 Champion

1948 Champion

1947 Commander

1948 Commander

1949 Commander

1942 Champion Custom club sedan

1946 Skyway Champion coupe

1942 President DeLuxstyle sedan-coupe

1947 Commander Regal DeLuxe 5-passenger coupe

1942 Commander Custom Cruising Sedan

1948 Commander Regal DeLuxe convertible

STUDEBAKER

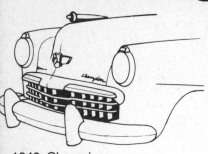

1949 Champion

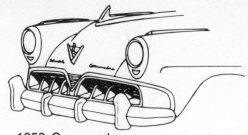

1950 Champion

1952 Commander

1950 Commander

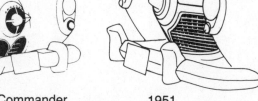

1951

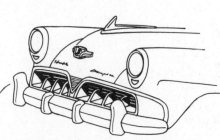

1952 Champion

1949 Commander DeLuxe 4-door sedan

1950 Commander Land Cruiser sedan

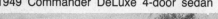

1951 Commander State Starlight coupe

1953 Commander Regal Starliner hardtop coupe

1953 Commander Regal Starliner hardtop coupe

1955 Commander Regal 4-door sedan

STUDEBAKER

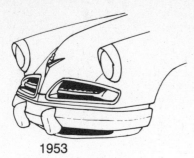
1953

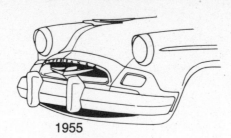
1955

1956 Hawk

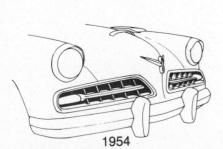
1954

1956 Champion, Commander, President

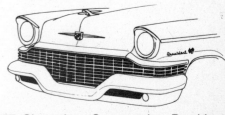
1957 Champion, Commander, President

1955 President State 4-door sedan

1955 Commander Regal Conestoga wagon

1956 Golden Hawk hardtop coupe

1956 Champion 2-door sedan

1957 President Classic 4-door sedan

1957 Golden Hawk hardtop coupe

STUDEBAKER

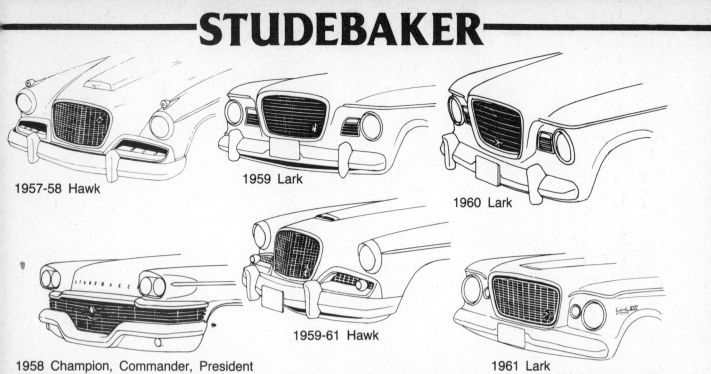

1957-58 Hawk

1959 Lark

1960 Lark

1958 Champion, Commander, President

1959-61 Hawk

1961 Lark

1957 Golden Hawk hardtop coupe

1958 President Starlight hardtop coupe

1959 Lark Regal 4-door sedan

1959 Silver Hawk coupe

1960 Lark Regal convertible

1961 Hawk coupe

1961 Lark Cruiser

1962 Gran Turismo Hawk

1963 Gran Turismo Hawk

1962 Lark

1963 Lark

1963 Avanti

1961 Lark Cruiser sedan

1962 Gran Turismo Hawk hardtop coupe (prototype)

1963 Lark Daytona hardtop coupe

1963 Avanti coupe

1963 Lark Daytona Wagonaire wagon

1964 Daytona Wagonaire wagon

STUDEBAKER

1964 Challenger, Commander

1964 Gran Turismo Hawk

1965

1964 Daytona, Cruiser

1964 Avanti

1966

1964 Avanti coupe

1964 Daytona hardtop coupe

1965 Commander 4-door sedan

1965 Daytona Sport sedan

1966 Cruiser sedan

1966 Daytona sport sedan

WILLYS

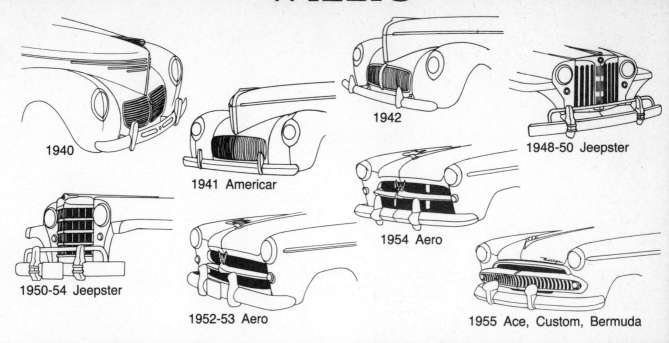

1940

1941 Americar

1942

1948-50 Jeepster

1950-54 Jeepster

1952-53 Aero

1954 Aero

1955 Ace, Custom, Bermuda

1940 Series 440 DeLuxe wagon

1948 Jeepster phaeton convertible

1950 Jeepster phaeton convertible

1952 Aero-Eagle hardtop coupe

1952 Aero-Wing 2-door sedan

1955 Bermuda hardtop coupe